Music Theory for Ukulele

Master the Essential Knowledge
with this Easy, Step-by-Step Method
for Beginner to Intermediate Players

by David Shipway

Music Theory for Ukulele
by David Shipway

Published by Headstock Books
headstockbooks.com

Cover images by Samuel Ramos and Jakob Owens.

Paperback ISBN: 978-1-914453-50-2
Hardcover ISBN: 978-1-914453-52-6 / 978-1-914453-53-3
Ebook ISBN: 978-1-914453-51-9

Acknowledgements

There are a few people I would like to thank for their help in producing this book.

First and foremost, my son James Shipway, who has been co-author, editor and publisher. James is a graduate of The Guitar Institute in London and also Leeds College of Music and now has a large following as a guitar teacher and author of a successful series of books and courses for guitar players.

His help has been invaluable in restraining my enthusiasm for the subject of this book and keeping explanations as concise and clear as possible and relevant to playing the ukulele.

I would also like to thank Aileen, James' wife, for putting everything together into a book and a special thank you to Sam, for stepping in to help out with proof-reading and formatting.

Thanks as well to those members of the Uke 'N Play ukulele group who acted as guinea pigs for some of the explanations and exercises in the book and encouraged me to keep at it.

So particular thanks to Jenny Norman, Rob Flexman, Jeannie O'Hea, David Luccioni and Ann Hayward but thanks also to all the group members and fellow musicians who add so much to life through the magic of making music.

Contents

Introduction

Hello and welcome to Music Theory for Ukulele!

Whether you have recently picked up a ukulele for the first time or have been playing for a while, this book will give you a crash course in the essential music theory I believe all players should know.

Like me, you probably started playing by learning some chords and following some song sheets. Hopefully you're having fun and enjoying the process just like I did…

But when I joined in with some other players, I soon found there was a whole new world of stuff out there to explore and understand. They seemed to speak a different language, a language made up of strange words like *major, minor, key, chord progression* …

I'm not going to lie, at first this language was mysterious and a little bit frightening and I was worried that only 'special' musicians could understand it.

I was wrong! With a little help, I soon discovered how *easy* it is to get a basic understanding of how music works. I also discovered how much this helped me become a better uke player! Suddenly I could understand the music I was playing on the uke. I could learn songs more easily, figure out chords faster and recognise common 'patterns' in music which songwriters use over and over again.

Since then, I've helped many uke players of all different levels better understand the music they play and the result is always the same: an increase in their confidence, playing skills and enjoyment of the ukulele!

Once *you* grasp the simple concepts, I am going to show you in this book you'll find the same thing happens to you. I'm pretty certain this book will be a turning point in your progress as a uke player.

And before you ask, don't worry, you'll be able to understand *everything* I'm going to show you in this book without needing to read music.

Sound good?

Then read on …

How Should You Use This Book?

For the best possible results with these 'first steps' in music theory I'd suggest these 5 simple tips:

1. **Start at the beginning and work through the chapters in order.** Even if you find the early material a bit basic, do go through it. This will make sure there are no gaps in your understanding which could hold you up later on. I've chosen to cover the absolute basics because I've found that *not* understanding basic concepts is the thing that holds most players up.

2. **Test yourself with the quiz at the end of each chapter**. This will make sure you understand each chapter fully before moving on. The chapters build on each other so it's important to grasp each one before tackling the next. You'll find the answers at the end of each chapter so that you can see how you did.

3. **Do the practical exercises**. There are various exercises to do throughout the book. These help you to see how the theory relates to the ukulele. There's no need to worry about reading music because we'll be using fretboard diagrams and chord boxes with clear explanations.

   For the more complex exercises, I've indicated in the book where there are online video demonstrations to help you play them.

   You'll find all the video demonstrations at:

   ## www.ukuleletheory.com

4. **Study each chapter more than once**. There's no rush! Take your time and study each chapter as many times as necessary until it becomes second nature.

5. **Look for examples of the concepts in this book when you listen to or play music**. Start to think about chord sequences and keys and try to analyse what is happening in a particular song or tune. If this sounds intimidating now, don't worry, it will soon be easy!

Ok, I think we're ready to get started!

So good luck and let's start *right* at the beginning...

Chapter 1:
The Musical Alphabet

Amazing though it may seem, all music is made from only **12 notes**!

These 12 notes are often called the *chromatic scale*. This sounds a bit scary and 'chromatic' can mean other things too in music, so I prefer to call the 12 notes the *'musical alphabet'*.

The **musical alphabet** is the basis of everything else I'm going to show you in this book so it's really important that you understand it early on.

Luckily, it's pretty simple to get to grips with.

Here's What You Need To Know About The Musical Alphabet

The 7 'Natural' Notes

There are **7** letter names used to name the notes in music. These are:

A, B, C, D, E, F and G

These letters describe 7 of the 12 notes in the musical alphabet. These 7 notes, just with letter names, are often called the **'natural'** notes.

Let's look at a diagram of the ukulele neck.

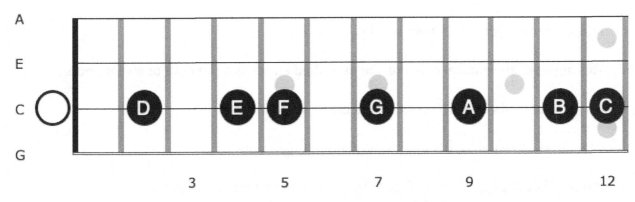

It shows the natural notes played along the C string (3rd string). The first note (C) is played using the open C string, then we play up the string to get the remainder of the natural notes.

Play them to see the natural notes in action.

So that's 7 of the notes in the musical alphabet, what about the remaining **5** notes?

'Sharps' and 'Flats'

The remaining **5** notes are the '*sharps*' and '*flats*'.

The symbol for sharp is **#** (e.g. the note 'C sharp' is written C#).

The symbol for flat is *b* (e.g. the note 'B flat' is written B*b*).

Sharps and flats sit *in between* the natural notes in the musical alphabet.

In a moment I'll be showing you some diagrams which will help you see this in action.

Now, something important to understand:

The notes between the natural notes have two possible names! They can be described using either their 'flat' or their 'sharp' name.

Some people get a bit confused by this, so let's clarify this idea before we move on.

In the musical alphabet there is one note sitting in between C and D. We could call it by its sharp name: **C#** (C sharp).

But we could also call it by its flat name: **D*b*** (D flat).

Whichever name we use, it is the same note!

Playing **C#** will sound exactly the same as playing **D*b*.**

Don't let this confuse you, just remember this simple rule:

The notes between the natural notes can be described either as a flat note or a sharp note.

So which name should you use? The flat name or the sharp name?

This depends on a few things, but don't worry about it right now.

It is not really that important, so we'll leave that explanation for another time.

The 7 natural notes plus the 5 sharps / flats, give us our complete musical alphabet.

If we write it out starting on A, it looks like this:

A - A#/B*b* - **B** - **C** - C#/D*b* - **D** - D#/E*b* - **E** - **F** - F#/G*b* - **G** - G#/A*b*

The 'Missing' Sharps and Flats

Now you might have noticed something strange:

There are some sharps and flats missing in places!

This is not a mistake; some natural notes do not have a sharp or flat note between them.

There is no sharp (#) or flat (*b*) note in between B and C *or* between E and F.

This is just the way our musical language has evolved over the centuries.

So, remember this:

There is no B# or C*b*.

There is no E# or F*b*.

Helping You 'See' The Musical Alphabet

Let's look at the 12 note musical alphabet on the piano keyboard (don't worry, you don't need to play the piano to get this!).

The way the piano is laid out makes it really easy to see the musical alphabet. Here it is starting on A:

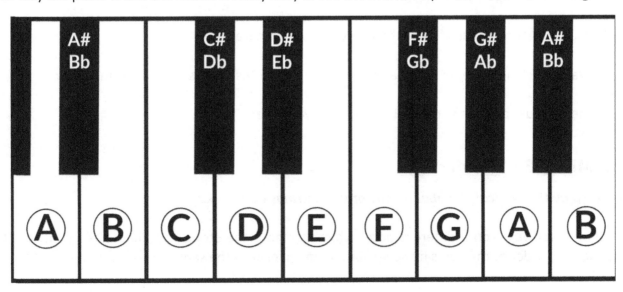

Remember we have 7 natural notes? These are the white keys: A B C D E F G.

The black keys are our **sharps** (#) and **flats** (b). Notice how there is **not** a black key between B and C or between E and F.

This is because, like we just saw, there is no B# / Cb or E# / Fb in the musical alphabet.

If we go back to our diagram of the ukulele neck, we can now see the complete musical alphabet shown along the C string.

I've only shown one possible name here for each sharp / flat, can you work out what the alternative names would be?

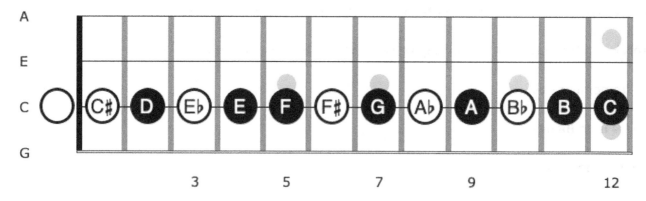

If you kept going along the string after the 12th fret, the sequence of notes would begin again and keep repeating until you ran out of frets!

Let's play it to check you understand this idea. We'll play it on the C or third string:

1. Start on the open 3rd string ...this is C

2. Play this string at each fret all the way up to the 12th fret

3. Name each note as you play it and remember, the notes always go in the same order

Well done, you just played the musical alphabet on your uke!

You Might Be Wondering...

Can you play the musical alphabet on any of the 4 strings on the uke?

Yes! It will just begin on a different note: whichever note the string you choose is tuned to. The sequence and order of the notes however would remain exactly the same.

What is a 'note' anyway?

A musical note is simply the sound of something vibrating. On different musical instruments, these 'vibrations' are caused in different ways.

On a ukulele notes are produced by the strings vibrating when plucked or strummed. Pressing down a string at any fret on our uke and plucking it creates a vibration. Depending on which fret we're pressing the string down at, the vibration will match one of the notes in the musical alphabet.

It's all to do with the tension of the string. The more we increase the tension in a string, the higher sounding the resulting note will be. The lower the tension on the string, the lower the note will sound.

Think of when you tune your uke: you tighten or loosen the string using the tuning pegs until each string is tuned to the desired note.

You say that there are only 12 notes but I can play many more than twelve notes on my ukulele!

Despite what it may look like there are only 12 notes on the ukulele!

It might *look* like there are more, but this is just because every different note can be found at several different locations on the neck.

If you want to see this for yourself, then be my guest!

Take a look at the diagram in Appendix 2 at the end of this book. It shows all the notes on the ukulele neck. Count them and you'll see it's just the same 12 notes played in multiple places!

And that's pretty much all you need to know about the musical alphabet!

In the next section we are going to look at the musical alphabet in action on the ukulele and learn about tones and semitones, but before we do, test yourself on the following questions, to make sure you have fully understood this section.

The musical alphabet is the foundation of everything else you are going to learn in this book, so it's important that you grasp everything in this chapter before you move on.

Good luck!

Now, Test Yourself On The Musical Alphabet!

1. The musical alphabet contains _____ notes.

2. The musical alphabet is also called the _____ scale.

3. The notes A, B, C, D, E, F and G are the _____ notes.

4. The symbol we use for a sharp is _____.

5. The symbol we use for a flat is _____.

6. There is no flat or sharp note in between the notes _____ and _____.

7. There is also no flat or sharp note in between the notes _____and_____.

8. The note in between G and A is _____ sharp or _____ flat.

9. Between D and E you get the note _____ or _____.

10. Here's the musical alphabet starting on C. Fill in the gaps. Use both the sharp and the flat name where applicable:

    C   C# / _   _   _ / _   _   _   _ / _   G   _ / _   _   _ / _   _   C

To find out how you did, check the answers on the next page!

How Did You Do?

1. *The musical alphabet contains **12** notes.*

2. *The musical alphabet is also called the **chromatic** scale.*

3. *The notes A, B, C, D, E, F and G are the **natural** notes.*

4. *The symbol we use for a sharp is **#**.*

5. *The symbol we use for a flat is **b**.*

6. *There is no flat or sharp note in between **B** and **C**.*

7. *There is also no flat or sharp note in between the notes **E** and **F**.*

8. *The note in between G and A is **G#** or **Ab**.*

9. *Between D and E you get the note **D#** or **Eb**.*

10. *Starting on C the musical alphabet looks like this:*

C   C#/Db   D   D#/Eb   E   F   F#/Gb   G   G#/Ab   A   A#/Bb   B   C

Chapter 2:
Tones and Semitones

Tones ...semitones ...half-steps ...whole-steps.

You may have heard these terms before, but do you know what they mean?

And how do they fit in with our musical alphabet?

Luckily, this is not hard to understand and is very easy to see on the ukulele.

A '*tone*' is a movement of **2 frets** on our uke. Sometimes a tone is also called a '*whole-step*'.

So, if you moved a note up **2 frets** along the neck, or down **2 frets**, you'd be moving it the distance of a **tone**.

Grab your uke and play the 1st string at the 3rd fret. This is the note C. Next play the note on the same string at the 5th fret. This is the note D.

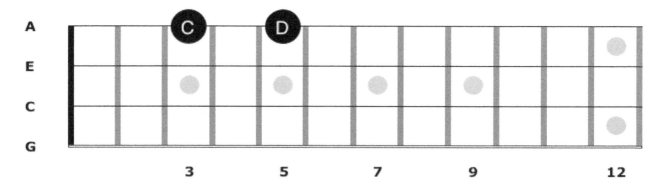

We have just moved C up 1 tone higher to D.

Let's play around with this some more. Try this simple exercise:

On the 1st string (or A string):

1. Play the note at the **3rd fret**. This is C.
2. Now move it up a tone to the **5th fret** to get D.
3. Next, move it up a tone to the **7th fret** to get E.
4. Finally, move it down **2 tones**, taking you back to the **3rd fret** where you began.

Now, still on the 1st string (or A string), play this and count:

```
1  2  3  4
C  D  E  C
```

If you play this twice you should recognise the beginning of the traditional tune *'Frère Jacques'*. The melody is made up from 3 notes, moving the distance of 1 tone or 2 tones:

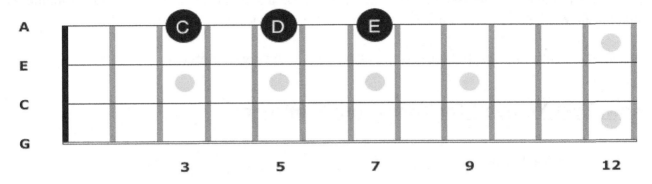

So now you know about **tones**!

A *'semitone'* is a movement of **half a tone**, or **1 fret**. A semitone is also called a *'half-step'*. Moving a semitone on the uke is like moving up or down **1 fret**.

Try this simple exercise:

1. Play the **open A** string.
2. Next play this string pressed down at the **1st fret**.
3. Now press it down at the **2nd fret**.
4. Keep moving it up **1 fret** at a time until you reach the **12th fret**.

You just played all 12 notes in the musical alphabet along the A string!

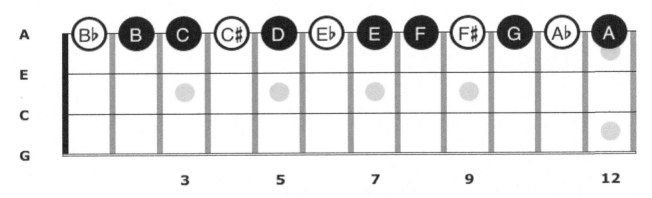

Notice how each time we go to the next note in the musical alphabet we are moving **1 fret** or a **semitone**. This is because each note in the sequence is a semitone apart.

Now, beginning up at the 12th fret, play back down the A string 1 fret at a time until you arrive back at the open string.

Each time you go down a semitone you land on the next note in the musical alphabet.

And that's most of what you need to know about **tones** and **semitones**!

We're now ready to put these together in the next chapter and make a major scale. Understanding the major scale will help you to understand a lot of the music you will play on your ukulele.

Test yourself with the quiz that follows and I'll see you in the next chapter!

Now, Test Yourself On Tones And Semitones!

1. A tone is a distance of _____ frets.

2. A semitone is a distance of _____ fret.

3. A tone can also be called a _____.

4. A semitone can also be called a _____.

To find out how you did, check the answers on the next page!

How Did You Do?

1. *A tone is a distance of **2** frets.*

2. *A semitone is a distance of **1** fret.*

3. *A tone can also be called a **whole-step**.*

4. *A semitone can also be called a **half-step**.*

Chapter 3:
The Major Scale

It's time to use our knowledge of tones and semitones to learn about one of the most important musical tools there is, the '**Major Scale**'.

First of all, what is a scale?

We'll define a scale as:

> *a set of notes we can use to create a particular musical sound or 'musical colour'*

Note the word *particular*. You see, there are many different scales used in music, giving us lots of different sounds. This explains why some music sounds uplifting and happy and other music sounds dark or scary.

The most important scale we need to understand as ukulele players is the **7** note Major Scale.

You Might Be Thinking...

'Hang on! I'm not interested in playing up and down scales on my uke, I want to play chords and songs I like! Why do I need to know all this scale stuff?'

Don't worry: we are not going to be endlessly playing up and down scales like you may have had to do in other music lessons!

Whether or not you play the major scale on your ukulele doesn't really matter, the point is that once you understand it you can make sense of chords, keys, chord sequences, songs and a lot more of the things you use when you play songs and music.

Later on in this book we'll discover how and why this works and you'll see just how useful the major scale is.

Ok, let's get back to the major scale now.

Grab your uke and do this quick exercise:

1. Play the **3rd string** as an **open string**. You're playing a C note.

2. Play the **3rd string** up a **tone** (that's **2 frets**, remember?) at the **2nd fret**.

3. Now move it up another **tone** to the **4th fret**.

4. Now move it up a **semitone** (that's **1 fret**, remember?) to the **5th fret**.

5. Now move it up a **tone**.

6. Next move it up another **tone**.

7. Move it up one more **tone**.

8. Go up a **semitone**.

That's it!

You should be up at the **12th** fret. You're actually back on the C note you began on, just one **octave** higher. An octave is the 'musical distance' from the beginning of the scale to the end. So, the two 'C' notes at either end of the scale would be described as being 'an octave apart'.

You just played a C major scale along the 3rd string on your uke. You can see this in the following diagram. It also shows you the names of the notes you played:

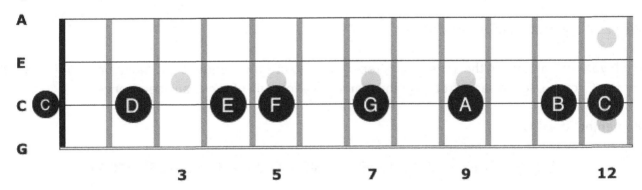

Ok, now go back to the beginning of this exercise and check what you have done.

Let's look at the pattern of tones and semitones you made when you did this simple exercise.

You began on the first note, then you went:

Up a tone
Up a tone
Up a semitone
Up a tone
Up a tone
Up a tone
Up a semitone

This is important: you see, the major scale is simply a sequence of tones and semitones arranged in a set order!

So, whatever you do, remember this formula:

TONE – TONE – SEMITONE – TONE – TONE – TONE – SEMITONE

The note you start the tone-semitone formula on determines which major scale you get.

You just started on a C note, so the major scale you got was the **C major scale**.

But if you had started on a D and followed the formula, you'd have got a **D major scale** instead.

Starting from the note A will give you the **A major scale** and so on ...

Remember this important fact: this starting note is called the '*root note*'.

Now, Test Yourself With These Simple Exercises!

Exercise 1:

Play an A major scale on your own!

Grab your uke and using the 1st string A, repeat the exact same sequence of movements you just did for the C scale. Use the same frets and the major scale formula of tones and semitones.

Remember it's this:

TONE – TONE – SEMITONE – TONE – TONE – TONE – SEMITONE

Play the pattern along the A string a few times to get familiar with it. Listen to the sound it makes as you go, I'll bet it sounds familiar! This is because major scales are used in so much of the music we hear from day-to-day.

Exercise 2:

Now for something a little more advanced! Look at the pattern of the A major scale along the A string.

Can you use your knowledge of the musical alphabet to work out the names of the notes you are playing?

Have a go and if necessary, write out the musical alphabet on a piece of paper to help you work it out.

Remember: the twelve notes in the musical alphabet are all a semitone apart so when you move a tone you will skip a note in the sequence of notes.

> **e.g.** a tone up from D puts you on E (you hop over the D#/E*b* in the sequence). A tone up from B puts you on C# (you skip over the C).

You don't need to learn all the notes in the scale, working them out in this way will just help you understand the major scale better.

Off you go!

You'll see the answer in a moment.

One Final Thing On The Major Scale ...

We can play a major scale starting on any of the notes in the musical alphabet. This gives us 12 possible major scales. Although some of these are very similar, no two major scales contain the exact same 7 notes.

All the major scales apart from the C major scale contain at least one flat (*b*) or sharp (#) note.

The G major scale for example contains an F#.

The F major scale contains a flat note: B*b*

Sometimes this confuses people, but the explanation is really quite simple.

When we follow the tone/semitone pattern starting from any root note, except C, we just happen to land on at least one sharp or flat note. This is just the way it works out and is why most major scales contain at least one flat or sharp note.

Go back to where you played the C major scale on the 3rd string. Look at the diagram giving you the note names and you'll see that there are no sharps or flats in this scale. It's just the way the pattern works.

But if we look at the **answer to Exercise 2** I gave you a moment ago you can see the A major scale actually contains 3 sharp (#) notes: C#, F# and G# as shown in the following diagram.

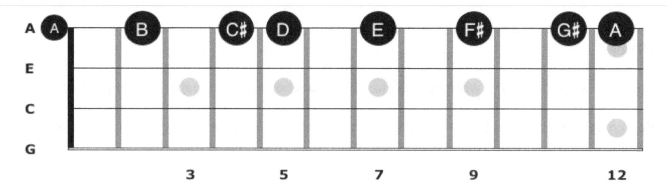

Now look at the diagram below.

It shows the notes which are *not* in the A major scale as white circles. These are the notes you 'hopped over' when you followed the tone/semitone formula starting on the open A string.

You can now see why you landed on some sharp notes more easily:

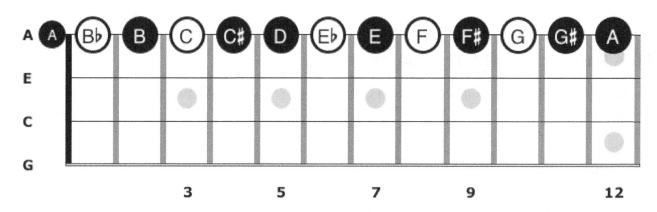

Ok, that's most of what you need to know about the major scale!

Now we can move on and see how the major scale is used to build all the chord shapes and chord sequences you are most likely playing on your uke. This is where your new knowledge will really start to pay off!

Before you move on, test yourself with the following questions and go back over anything you're not sure about.

The information in this chapter is important so answer the questions, check your answers, recap on anything you need to …and I'll see you again in the next chapter.

Now, Test Yourself On The Major Scale!

1. The major scale contains _____ notes.

2. The formula of tones and semitones used to get a major scale is:

   _____

3. The note we start the formula on is often called the _____ note.

4. Can the pattern of tones/semitones be changed? _____

5. How many possible major scales are there? _____

6. All major scales apart from the C major scale contain at least one _____ or _____ note.

7. When you've played through the scale you end up on the starting note one _____ higher.

To find out how you did, check the answers on the next page!

How Did You Do?

1. *The major scale contains **7** notes.*

2. *The formula of tones and semitones used to get a major scale is:*

TONE - TONE - SEMITONE - TONE - TONE - TONE - SEMITONE

3. *The note we start the formula on is often called the **root** note.*

4. ***No, the pattern of tones/semitones cannot be changed.** It must stay the same or the scale is not a major scale anymore.*

5. *There are **12** major scales, one for each note of the musical alphabet.*

6. *All major scales apart from the C major scale contain at least one **sharp** or **flat** note.*

7. *When you've played through the scale you end up on the starting note one **octave** higher.*

Chapter 4:
Building Chords –
Major and Minor Triads

A chord is probably the first thing you learned when starting out on your uke. Quite likely it was a C chord.

Even though we use chords a lot, many uke players don't really know what a chord actually is and whilst it's possible to play the uke without knowing much about the chords you use, a little bit of knowledge means you can easily understand most of the music you play. This helps you become a better player.

The simplest chords to understand are called triads. Let's begin by looking at these.

First of all, what actually is a chord?

Think of a chord as:

a group of notes played together to give a certain sound

The two most common chords you'll see are the **major** and **minor** chord.

Think of these as two different types, or 'flavour' of chord with a different sound.

Major chords have a 'happy', uplifting and positive sound. When talking about a major chord we often just use the letter part of the chord's full name. In other words:

'**G major**' is normally just called '**G**'.

'**A major**' is normally just called '**A**'.

Minor chords give us a sadder, more sombre sound. We'll look at an example of this later on in this chapter.

Let's go back to triads. A triad is simply:

a chord which is made up of 3 notes

You've probably been playing triads on your uke already, maybe without knowing it! You see, most common ukulele chords contain just 3 notes and are therefore triads.

'But hang on!' you're thinking, 'My uke has 4 strings, surely a chord on the uke contains 4 notes?'

Nope! You might be playing 4 strings in a chord but most of the time you are only playing 3 notes, one of the notes is simply played more than once in the chord shape.

This chord box shows you the notes you are playing when you strum this common C chord:

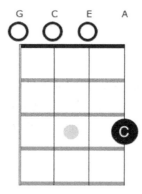

It only contains **3** notes: notes C, E and G. The C is played twice giving us a 4-string chord.

Look at this A minor chord. It also contains **3** notes. Can you spot which note is doubled in this chord?

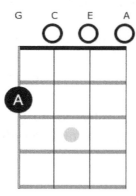

If a triad is a chord containing **3** notes and most of the chords you use on your ukulele are probably triads, you might be wondering where these triads actually come from.

Let's look at this next...

Building A Major Triad

This is where your knowledge of the major scale comes in useful.

To make a '*major triad*' simply group together the first note (root), 3rd note and 5th note of any major scale.

So, the formula looks like this:

Root + 3rd + 5th = Major Triad

Let's look at how this works in practice. Here are the notes of the C Major scale:

C D E F G A B

Can you work out the C major triad?

If you grouped together C (root) + E (3rd) + G (5th) you are absolutely right!

Check the C chord diagram we saw a moment ago and you'll see these 3 notes making up the chord.

This process of stacking the 1st (root), 3rd and 5th notes from a major scale to get a major triad works for all major scales, of which, (as you already know) there are 12.

These diagrams show us two ways we can play a C chord on the uke. Examine the notes shown and see if they fit the **root + 3rd + 5th** formula we just saw:

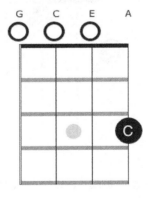

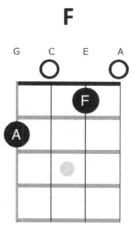

This shows us that no matter which shape we use to play a particular chord, the notes in the chord will always be the same (if the notes changed it would not be the same chord!).

You can also see how the notes don't have to be played in any set order and that the same chord can be created at different places along the neck of the uke.

Ok, now let's see how you get on with these exercises:

Exercise 1

1. Look at the chord box below showing you how to play an **F** chord:

F

2. Go back to our musical alphabet and write out the **F major scale**. Use the Tone-Tone-Semitone-Tone-Tone-Tone-Semitone formula to work out the notes in the scale.
3. Identify the **root + 3rd + 5th** from the scale.
4. Does your answer match the notes in the chord shape you were just given?

Exercise 2

1. Look at the chord box below showing you how to play a **G** chord:

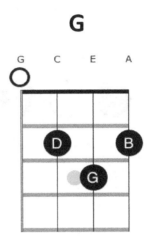

2. Go back to the musical alphabet and write out the notes in the **G major scale** using the formula for the major scale (tone-tone-semitone-tone-tone-tone-semitone).
3. Find the **root, 3rd and 5th** from the scale to get the notes in the **G major triad**.
4. Does your answer match the notes in the G chord shape you were just given?

Take your time with these exercises and don't worry if you don't get them both right the first time. Go step-by-step through them again until you have that light-bulb moment when it all makes perfect sense!

What Is A Minor Triad?

The other common form of triad is the '*minor triad*'. This is like a major triad but there is one very important difference.

The 1st (root), the 3rd and the 5th notes are grouped together as before but the **3rd is flattened** by a semitone.

What do we mean by *flatten*?

To *flatten* a note, lower it by a semitone. On the ukulele this simply means we move it down **1 fret**.

Grab your uke and play the note at the 2nd fret on the 3rd string (you're playing D).

Now move the note down 1 fret to the 1st fret. You just flattened it, changing the note from D to D flat (written as D*b*). Don't forget D*b* is the same note as C#.

So, flattening a note simply means moving it down a fret or a semitone.

Here is the diagram you saw earlier showing you the musical alphabet written out on the C string:

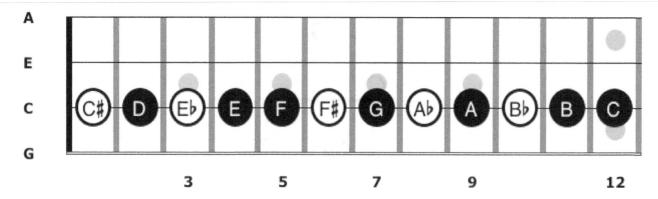

Notice how the following applies:

Flatten A and you get A*b*

Flatten C and you get B

Flatten B and you get B*b*

Now that you know what it means to flatten a note by a semitone, let's return to our minor triad.

To build a minor triad take the 1st (root), the 3rd and the 5th notes from the major scale. Then flatten the 3rd by a semitone. This gives us a *flattened 3rd*, normally written as *b*3rd or *b*3.

Just flattening one note might not seem like much, but it makes a big difference to the sound of the triad!

Let's see this in action, here's an A major triad played on the uke:

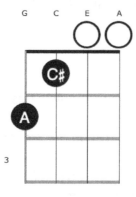

It contains the notes A, C# and E. This is because these are the 1st, 3rd and 5th notes in the A major scale:

A B **C#** D **E** F# G#

Notice how the 3rd (C#) is played on the 3rd string at the 1st fret.

Now remove your first finger from the 1st fret on the 3rd string. Doing this moves the 3rd of the chord (C#) down a semitone to the open string giving the note C. This changes the 3rd into a flattened 3rd, transforming our A major triad into A minor.

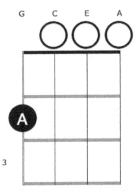

Play the two chord shapes, putting your 1st finger on and off to hear the difference the flattened 3rd makes to the sound of the chord.

Let's compare the two triads one more time:

A major triad = **A** (root) + **C#** (3rd) + **E** (5th)

A minor triad = **A** (root) + **C** (b3rd) + **E** (5th)

Look at the following chord shapes for playing D and D minor. Can you see the same thing happening here? (Hint: the 3rd of D is F#!)

D

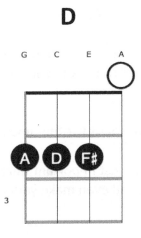

Dm

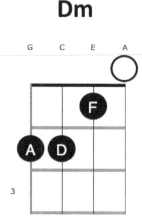

You've probably been using all these chord shapes a lot in the songs you play on your uke, but now you understand *why* they are the way they are!

Let's wrap up our look at triads with a quick summary ...

The formula for creating a **major triad** is the **1st** + **3rd** + **5th** notes from a major scale.

The formula for creating a **minor triad** is the **1st** + **b3rd** + **5th** notes from a major scale.

You Might Be Thinking...

We've talked a lot about major scales. Is there such a thing as a minor scale?

Yes, absolutely! There are a few types of minor scale, but the one thing they all have in common is the flattened 3rd (*b*3).

You see, the *b*3rd is the note that defines a scale or chord as being minor and anything 'minor' will contain a *b*3.

Are major and minor the only kind of triads there are?

No, there are others, but you won't see them often and don't need to know the theory behind them for now. Just understand major and minor triads and you'll be fine for playing most of the music you'll probably ever play.

That's all you really need to know about triads for the time being.

Coming in the next chapter is one of the most important things you need to know about on the uke. It helps you play songs, understand songs and even make your own songs: keys!

<u>Now, Test Yourself On Triads!</u>

1. Triads are chords containing _____ notes.

2. What is the formula for a major triad?

   _____

3. What is the formula for a minor triad?

   _____

4. What is the only difference between a major and minor triad?

   _____

5. The notes in the D major scale are: D E F# G A B C#

   What are the notes in a D major triad?   _____

   What are the notes in a D minor triad?   _____

6. The notes in the B*b* major scale are: B*b* C D E*b* F G A

   What are the notes in a B*b* major triad?   _____

   What are the notes in a B*b* minor triad?   _____

To find out how you did, check the answers on the next page!

How Did You Do?

1. *Triads are chords containing **3** notes.*

2. *The formula for a major triad is **root + 3rd + 5th** from a major scale.*

3. *The formula for a minor triad is **root + b3rd + 5th** from a major scale.*

4. *The only difference between a major and minor triad is the **flattened 3rd** in the minor triad.*

5. *The notes in a D major triad are **D F# and A**.*

   *The notes in a D minor triad are **D F and A**.*

6. *The notes in a Bb major triad are **Bb D and F**.*

   *The notes in a Bb minor triad are **Bb Db and F**.*

Chapter 5:
Major Keys (Part 1)

So far, we have looked at notes and the way that 12 notes form the musical alphabet. We've also seen how to use these notes to create major scales as well as major and minor chords or triads.

You now have enough knowledge to look at one of the most important and useful musical concepts you need to know: *'keys'*.

Imagine you are strumming a song with some fellow uke players, following the chords given on your song sheet.

Suddenly uke player 1 asks:

'What key is this song in?'

Uke player 2 answers:

'It's in the key of F major.'

Most of the uke players in the room would probably be totally baffled by this question!

The good news is that after reading this chapter you won't be one of them...

What Is A Key?

Let's begin by looking at what a key is. I like to use this simple definition:

The 'key' a song is in tells you what scale the 'raw material' used in the song comes from

We could define 'raw material' as the notes making up the melody or tune the singer is singing and the notes in the chords played in the song's chord sequence.

So, when the musician in the conversation above says the song is 'in the key of F major', he means:

All the notes sung in the melody of this song...

All the notes contained in the chords you use to play the song...

The notes in any fingerpicking patterns you might play in the song ...

And anything else you hear in it...

All use the 7 notes found in the F major scale.

The F major scale is like the 'source' of everything in the song.

In a nutshell, that's what a key is. Sometimes it does get a little more complicated than this, but for now this simple explanation will do the job.

Let's look at how we use the notes from a major scale to build chord families. Once you get the hang of this idea, you'll suddenly be able to make sense of chord sequences and song structures like never before!

Chord Families

We know that the major scale contains **7** notes.

What's really great is that we can do something with these **7** notes to make **7 chords**. Think of these 7 chords as a '***chord family***' and think of the scale they come from as the '***parent scale***'.

Let's look at an example.

If we take the C major scale as our **parent scale,** we get the following 7 chords in the C major chord family:

C	Dm	Em	F	G	Am	B diminished

Note: major chords are written with their letter names only: 'C major' written as **C**, 'G major' written as **G** and so on.

These 7 chords are the chord family which come from the C major scale.

We could also say that these chords are the *chords in the key of C*.

We'll be seeing in a moment why this chord family stuff is *so* useful.

If you've been playing a little while you might have some questions about this, questions like:

'When I play in C I often play a G7 chord. Why isn't it shown in the chord family?'

'What on earth is a Bdim (diminished) chord? I've never seen that in a song in C'.

These are good questions but don't worry about them for now, we'll be answering these later in this book. Back to our C major chord family …

Don't question *why* these are the chords in the key of C, we'll be looking at that in the next chapter. Just know that these chords can be traced back to the notes in the C major scale. The C major scale is the *parent scale*.

Because these chords are in the same 'chord family' and come from the same parent scale, they will all sound 'good' together when we mix them up.

So, when most people write a song, they're not just sticking chords together randomly. They know what key their song is in and which chords are in the chord family for that key. Using these chords, they can then construct a chord sequence for their song.

It could be:

C	G	Am	F	C	G	F	C

(Play this using any chord shapes you know to hear how it sounds. See the chord reference section at the back of this book if you need help with chord shapes).

Alternatively, our imaginary composer might try a different chord sequence:

C	Dm	F	G	Am	F	G	G

(Play this one and hear the sound!).

There are hundreds more possible chord combinations and which one is used is up to the person writing the song, but you can hopefully hear how these chords sound musical and natural when played together. This is because they come from a common source: the parent scale of C major.

Let's do a little experiment - it's a bit of nonsense but it makes a very clear point!

Play the chords below in a sequence from left to right. Play them with 4 strums per chord for now:

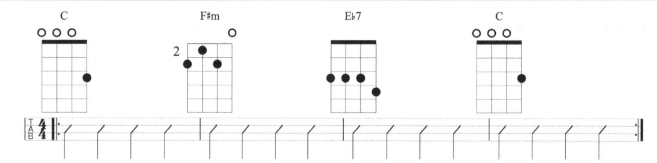

Sounds a bit weird doesn't it?

This is because these chords don't belong in a family together. I'd be very surprised to hear them used together in a song and personally, I wouldn't buy the record!

Let's summarise what we've seen so far in this chapter:

The parent major scale being used and the chord family derived from it, define which major key a piece of music is in.

So, in a song in the key of C you can expect to hear notes and chords derived from the 'parent' scale: C major.

These notes will make up the melody itself and will be contained in the chords used in the accompaniment as well as being used for intros, solos and anything else we hear in the song.

Now You Might Be Wondering...

How many major keys are there?

Because we can make 12 major scales from our 12 note musical alphabet, there are 12 possible major keys. Each one has its own unique chord family containing 7 chords.

As ukulele players, we only tend to use about half of these keys on a regular basis. This is because the chord fingerings can get more difficult in some keys and also because some chord families can be played more easily on the lower frets and have a fuller sound than those using higher fret positions.

The diagram below only shows the chord families for the most commonly used keys. However, you can find a full table at the end of the book if you wish to explore this in more detail.

KEY	I	II	III	IV	V	VI	VII
C	C	Dm	Em	F	G	Am	Bdim
F	F	Gm	Am	B*b*	C	Dm	Edim
G	G	Am	Bm	C	D	Em	F#dim
B*b*	B*b*	Cm	Dm	E*b*	F	Gm	Adim
D	D	Em	F#m	G	A	Bm	C#dim
A	A	Bm	C#m	D	E	F#m	G#dim
E	E	F#m	G#m	A	B	C#m	D#dim

What's With The Roman Numerals?

What are all those weird Roman numerals along the top all about?

Glad you asked: these are *incredibly* useful!

Along the top row of the chord family table you can see *Roman numerals* for the numbers 1-7. Here are the numbers applied just to the key of C. The more familiar 'Arabic' numbers we use every day are also shown to make it clearer:

I	II	III	IV	V	VI	VII
1	2	3	4	5	6	7
C	Dm	Em	F	G	Am	Bdim

Why are these numbers important?

It's because these numbers are often how musicians refer to the chords in a chord sequence.

Let's take a quick look at this...

In the key of **C**: chord **I** is **C**, chord **IV** is **F** and chord **V** is **G**.

I	II	III	IV	V	VI	VII
C	Dm	Em	**F**	**G**	Am	Bdim

Grab your uke and play the following using any chord shapes you know:

$$|: C \mid F \mid G \mid G :|$$

Done it?

If so, then you just played a **I-IV-V** chord sequence in the key of C.

This is because you played the chords with those numbers in that particular order.

If you'd played this one instead it would be called **I-V-IV**:

$$|: C \mid G \mid F \mid F :|$$

Play it and hear the difference in sound.

Let's sneak a minor chord in there now. Play this chord progression. It could be called **I-VI-IV-V**:

$$|: C \mid Am \mid F \mid G :|$$

Final example: here's a **I-II-V-IV** chord sequence in the key of **C**:

$$|: C \mid Dm \mid G \mid F :|$$

Hopefully, this all makes sense! Refer back to the key of C table if you need to clarify why we are using these numbers for each chord.

If you understand this concept, then you've taken a big step forward when it comes to understanding music and songs. You see, instead of thinking of a chord progression as a bunch of random chords strung together ...

You can think of them as a sequence or pattern of numbers, with each number referring to that number chord in the key you are in.

This simple concept makes it possible for you to do amazing things with chord progressions!

Changing Keys Quickly And Easily

Using Roman numerals to understand chord progressions is great... but it gets even better!

Imagine this ...

You are strumming a song with some fellow uke players following the chords given on your song sheet. The chords are:

|: G | Em | C | D :|

Suddenly the person singing says:

'Hang on, I can't sing it in this key, it's too high in places. Let's try it in a different key. Instead of G, let's take it down to the key of F.'

Most of the other players probably wouldn't have a clue where to even start with this ...

But because you know about chord families: it's easy!

Step 1: Work Out the Key and Number Sequence!

You look at the chords and figure out that they are **I-VI-IV-V** in the key of G:

I	II	III	IV	V	VI	VII
G	Am	Bm	C	D	Em	F#dim

Step 2: Use the Numbers to Find the Chords in the New Key!

We know that the chords will change when we change key ...but what will they become?

We said the sequence was **I-VI-IV-V** in the key of G. So now, find chords **I**, **VI**, **IV** and **V** in the new key: **F**

I	II	III	IV	V	VI	VII
F	Gm	Am	**Bb**	**C**	**Dm**	Edim

Step 3: Play Them in the Right Order and You're Done!

Now you know what the chords are, play the new chord progression:

$$|: F | Dm | Bb | C :|$$

And that's it: you just changed the key of the chord progression.

Hopefully now the singer can sing it more easily and if not, you now know how to change it into yet another key until they find the one they're happiest in!

So now you know why thinking of chord progressions in the way I've explained it is so useful. It helps you understand chord progressions and songs, change things into new keys quickly and easily and much more which you've yet to discover…

You Might Be Wondering…

Some keys share some of the same chords …is this right?

Well spotted, there is an 'overlap' of chords between keys, sometimes more than others. The keys of C and F share 4 chords for example. They are in different positions in the table and do a different musical 'job' in each key.

Don't let this confuse you. For now, just study the table and try to find examples of 'shared' chords. We'll look at this more closely when we come to examine some common chord progressions later on.

Can a song use a chord that's not in the chord family?

Yes, this does often happen.

Sometimes it sounds more interesting to take a 'detour' outside the key to get a different sound. There is normally still some relationship between the chords being used, even if some of them don't belong in the chord family. Again, more on this later.

Let's Experiment With Chord Families!

Before we end this chapter try this practical exercise:

1. Choose a key on the chord/key chart.
2. Take some of the chords in that key and play them together (ignore the diminished chord for the time being).
3. Hear how they 'fit' together well. This is because they're all in the same chord family.
4. Try putting them in different orders to create a simple chord sequence which sounds good to you.
5. Can you work out the number pattern of your chord sequences using the Roman numerals along the top of the table?

Doing this will help you see how useful your new understanding of keys can be!

And that's most of what you need to know to have a basic understanding of major keys …

Study everything in this chapter. Having a 'big picture' understanding of what a key is will make the theory coming up in the next chapter *way* easier to understand.

Also, remember to test yourself using the questions that follow and check the answers to make sure you understand everything.

When you're ready I'll see you in the next chapter where we're going to break down the idea of a key and look at where this family of 7 chords actually comes from.

Good luck and see you in the next chapter!

Now, Test Yourself On Major Keys!

1. What key a song is in tells you what _____ the 'raw material' used in the song comes from.

2. If a song is in the key of A major then all the notes making up the melody, bassline and the notes making up the chords played will be contained in the _____ scale.

3. There are _____ major keys in total.

4. Each key has a 'chord family' containing _____ chords.

5. The scale these chords come from is often called the _____.

6. Chord progressions can be described as number patterns using the _____ for each chord.

To find out how you did, check the answers on the next page!

How Did You Do?

1. *What key a song is in tells you what **scale** the 'raw material' used in the song comes from.*

2. *If a song is in the key of A major then all the notes making up the melody, bassline and the notes making up the chords played will be contained in the **A major** scale.*

3. *There are **12** major keys.*

4. *Each key has a 'chord family' containing **7** chords.*

5. *The scale these chords come from is often called the **parent scale**.*

6. *Chord progressions can be described as number patterns using the **Roman numerals** for each chord.*

Chapter 6:
Major Keys (Part 2):
Building the Chord Family

In the last chapter we took a big picture view of major keys.

We had this simple definition of a key:

The 'key' a song is in tells you what scale the 'raw material' used in the song comes from

So, if you had a song in the key of C major:

The melody of the song, the chords played in the song's chord sequence, the bassline, any intros, solos or anything else...

Would be using only the 7 notes found in the C major scale.

You also saw how each key has a 'chord family' of 7 chords for composing chord sequences in that key and how the 'parent scale' can be used to play melodies over these chords.

Now it's time to look at the theory behind this concept and discover where chord families actually come from. This will give you a thorough understanding of major keys.

There's quite a lot in this chapter, but it's really important stuff. So, make yourself comfortable and let's begin ...

Building Chord Families From Major Scales

We're going to use the C major scale for this lesson and I'll show you how we create the C major 'chord family'.

I'll take you step by step through the process of building a chord family. By the end of this lesson you'll understand something which has confused many ukulele players for years!

Before we start...

Back in Chapter 4 we 'stacked' the notes in the scale to build major and minor triads. We're going to be using that knowledge now, so if you need a reminder of how it works have a quick re-read of that chapter!

Step 1: Build a triad on the *root* of the scale

Build a triad starting on the root of the C scale: **C**

C D **E** F **G** A B

This gives us the notes **C E G**.

You can see this is the **root + 3rd + 5th** of the scale.

Root + 3rd + 5th is the formula for a **major triad**, so the chord is **C** or **C major**.

Look at the C chord shape given here.

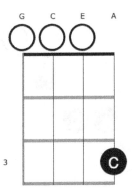

You can see how it contains the notes we just said made up the C major triad.

In conclusion, **C is the first chord** in the chord family or 'key' of C major.

Step 2: Build a triad on the *2nd* of the scale

Now we're going to do the same thing starting on the next note in the scale. We build a triad starting on the 2nd note: **D**. So, D will be the root note of our new triad.

C **D** E **F** G **A** B

This gives us the notes **D F A**.

This will be some kind of D triad as it has D as its root note.

But is it D major, D minor ...or something else entirely?

To find out what this chord is, we need to *compare* it to the notes in the D major scale. Then we can see if it contains a *b*5th, a *b*3rd or whatever and use this information to determine what kind of chord it is.

The D major scale is:

D E F# G A B C#

The notes in a D major triad would be **D F# A** - but that's **not** what we've got in our triad (D F A). We have an F instead of F# and this is the flattened 3rd of the D scale.

So, our triad is the **root + *b*3rd + 5th** of the D scale.

Root + *b*3rd + 5th is the formula for a **minor triad**, so the chord is **D minor**.

Don't forget that each triad chord we create is based on our starting note or root. Look at the chord diagram for Dm below.

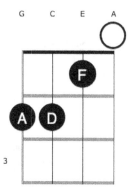

If you look at the notes which make up this Dm chord you will see it's a triad made up from the notes **D, F** and **A**.

Play the chord and have a look at the notes you are actually playing: it'll help everything make sense.

So **Dm is the second chord** in the chord family or 'key' of C major.

Sometimes people find this step a little confusing! If so, go over it a few more times before you move on.

Step 3: Build a triad on the *3rd* of the scale

Now build a triad starting on the 3rd of the scale: **E**

C D **E** F **G** A **B**

This gives us the notes **E G B**.

To find out what this chord is, we need to compare it to the notes in the E major scale. Then we can discover its formula and figure out if it's major, minor, or something else!

The E major scale is:

E F# G# A B C# D#

The notes in an E major triad would be **E G# B** - but that's **not** what we've got in our triad (E G B). We've got G instead of G# and this is the flattened 3rd of the E scale.

So, our triad is the **root + *b*3rd + 5th** of the E scale.

Root + *b*3rd + 5th is the formula for a **minor triad**, so the chord is **E minor**.

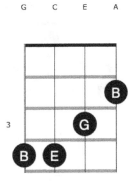

So **Em is the third chord** in the chord family or 'key' of C major.

We now have 3 chords in the C major chord family: **C**, **Dm** and **Em**

Let's carry on building chords from the C major scale.

Step 4: Build a triad on the *4th* of the scale

Now build a triad starting on the 4th of the scale: **F**

Let's extend the scale into another octave to make it clearer to see:

C D E **F** G **A** B **C** D E F G A B

This gives us the notes **F A C**.

To find out what this chord is we need to compare it to the notes in the F major scale.

The F major scale is:

F G A B*b* C D E

The notes in an F major triad are **F A C** and that's exactly what we've got in our F triad which came from the C major scale.

So, our triad is the **root + 3rd + 5th** giving us an **F major** chord.

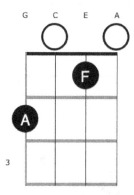

So, **F is the 4th chord** in the chord family or 'key' of C major.

Step 5: Build a triad on the *5th* of the scale

Now build a triad starting on the 5th of the scale: **G**

C D E F **G** A **B** C **D** E F G A B

This gives us the notes **G B D**.

To find out what this chord is we need to compare it to the notes in the G major scale.

The G major scale is:

G A B C D E F#

The notes in a G major triad are **G B D**, exactly the same as in the G triad which came from the C major scale.

So, our triad is the **root + 3rd + 5th** of the G scale, giving us a **G major** chord.

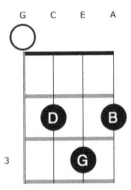

G is the 5th chord in the chord family or 'key' of C major.

Step 6: Build a triad on the 6th of the scale

Next build a triad starting on the 6th of the scale: **A**

C D E F G **A** B **C** D **E** F G A B

This gives us the notes **A C E**.

As before, we must compare it to the notes in the A major scale to figure out what kind of chord it is.

The A major scale is:

A B C# D E F# G#

The notes in an A major triad would be A C# E - **not** what we've got in our triad (A C E). We've got C instead of C#.

C is the flattened 3rd of the A scale.

So, our triad is the **root + b3rd + 5th** of the A scale.

This is the formula for a **minor triad**, making the chord **A minor**.

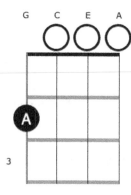

So **Am is the 6th chord** in the chord family or 'key' of C major.

Step 7: Build a triad on the 7th of the scale

The process for the 7th note triad is exactly the same as we have already seen in steps 1-6 but the outcome is slightly different as you will soon see.

For now, don't worry too much about the 'technical aspects' of this triad, just concentrate on understanding the process of how we arrive at it and how it gives us the seventh chord in our C chord family.

Build a triad starting on the 7th note of the scale: **B**

C D E F G A **B** C **D** E **F** G A B

This gives us the notes **B D F**.

As before, compare it to the notes in the B major scale to figure out what kind of chord it is.

The B major scale is:

B C# D# E F# G# A#

The notes in a B major triad would be B D# F# - **not** what we've got in our triad (B D F).

We've got a flattened 3rd (D), but we've also got a *flattened 5th* (F)!

So, our triad is the **root + *b*3rd + *b*5th** of the B scale.

We haven't seen this kind of triad yet, but **root + *b*3rd + *b*5th** is the formula for a **diminished triad.**

Now you may not see a diminished chord very often in your song book, but this particular triad has a special quality and forms the greater part of a very important type of chord used all the time by ukulele players.

Let me show you what I mean. Study the chord diagram below, it's a B diminished triad using the notes B D F taken from our C scale. Grab your uke and play strings 1, 2 and 3 as a chord leaving off string 4.

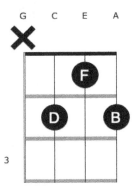

Now play the triad again followed by a C chord. Pay particular attention to the 1st string as you do this.

Can you hear how B diminished 'pulls' you back home to the I chord: C?

This is one of the strongest sounds in music and is *very* common in all kinds of music.

If you've been playing a while you will have noticed how the B diminished triad is very like this common G7 chord shape:

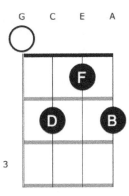

This is because diminished triads and dominant7 chords like G7, A7 or D7 are very closely related. We'll be learning more about dominant7 chords later on.

For now, just remember that **B diminished is the 7th chord** in the chord family or 'key' of C major.

The Story So Far ...

Ok, you can see that by building a triad starting on each note of the C major scale we get a set of 7 chords.

These chords are the 'chord family' which comes from the C major scale.

The process we've just seen is where chord families actually come from.

Let's carry on ...

More On Roman Numerals...

You'll remember in the last chapter we numbered the chords in the chord families with *Roman numerals*.

This gives us:

I	II	III	IV	V	VI	VII
1	2	3	4	5	6	7
C	Dm	Em	F	G	Am	Bdim

We saw how we can use this system to describe the chords in a key as a 'number', for example in the key of C:

E minor is chord **III** ('chord three')

G major is chord **V** ('chord five')

And so on...

The 'Magic Formula' For Getting *All* The Chords In *Any* Key!

Imagine if you could instantly recall what all the chords were in every single key.

It'd be amazing huh?

Well, the good news is that with what you've learned so far in this chapter you can easily learn to do exactly that!

Let's take the lessons learned from the C major scale and see how it can be easily applied to all the major scales to get all the chords in every key (it's way easier than you think!).

We need to look at the 'type' of chord we get on each note. This could also be called the 'quality' of the chord (i.e. whether it's major, minor or diminished).

If we look at the chords in the key of C we can see how:

I, IV and **V** are **major**

I	II	III	IV	V	VI	VII
MAJOR	MINOR	MINOR	**MAJOR**	**MAJOR**	MINOR	DIMINISHED

II, III and **VI** are **minor**

I	II	III	IV	V	VI	VII
MAJOR	**MINOR**	**MINOR**	MAJOR	MAJOR	**MINOR**	DIMINISHED

Chord **VII** is **diminished**

I	II	III	IV	V	VI	VII
MAJOR	MINOR	MINOR	MAJOR	MAJOR	MINOR	**DIMINISHED**

In summary, the chord family looks like this:

I	II	III	IV	V	VI	VII
MAJOR	MINOR	MINOR	MAJOR	MAJOR	MINOR	DIMINISHED

When we were working with these Roman numerals in the last chapter you may have noticed this formula... if so well done!

Let's look at this concept in more detail now and find out how we can use it.

This 'recipe' of Roman numerals and chord types can be applied to any of the other major scales to get the chords in that key too.

Let's look at how this works.

Look at the 'pattern' of chord types in the table we just looked at.

When we superimpose this 'pattern' on top of the notes in any other major scale it instantly tells us the chords in that key as well! All you need to know are the notes in the major scale in question.

A few examples might be useful here…

Example 1:

The **F** major scale is:

Root	2nd	3rd	4th	5th	6th	7th
F	G	A	B*b*	C	D	E

Apply the 'recipe' or chord pattern to these notes:

I	II	III	IV	V	VI	VII
MAJOR	MINOR	MINOR	MAJOR	MAJOR	MINOR	DIMINISHED
F	G	A	B*b*	C	D	E

And we get the chord family for the key of F:

I	II	III	IV	V	VI	VII
F	Gm	Am	B*b*	C	Dm	Edim

Example 2:

The **A** major scale is:

Root	2nd	3rd	4th	5th	6th	7th
A	B	C#	D	E	F#	G#

Apply the 'recipe' or chord pattern to these notes:

I	II	III	IV	V	VI	VII
MAJOR	MINOR	MINOR	MAJOR	MAJOR	MINOR	DIMINISHED
A	B	C#	D	E	F#	G#

And you get the chord family for the key of A major:

I	II	III	IV	V	VI	VII
A	Bm	C#m	D	E	F#m	G#dim

Just to be clear, this trick works for **every** major scale. So, you can use it to work out the chords in every major key (awesome, eh?).

Even better, I've done the hard work for you!

Look at the **chord / key chart** in the previous chapter to see the most common ukulele keys laid out in this way. To see the chords in every key, refer to the table in Appendix 1.

Now you know what you need to know about major keys and where they come from.

Phew!

That was a pretty jam-packed chapter, so don't worry if you didn't get it all the first time. Do take the time to study and digest this material because it is *invaluable*. I can't overstate how important it is!

It helps you:

- Understand songs and chord sequences
- Work out how to play other people's songs just by listening
- Write better music of your own
- Learn and remember songs more easily …

…and there are *loads* more awesome benefits as well!

So, learn the theory.

Study (maybe even *memorise*) the chords in the common keys ...

...then test yourself using the questions that follow.

Any time you invest in really nailing your understanding of keys will pay you back many times over in the future, so dig in and master this crucial topic!

Now, Test Yourself On Major Keys!

1. In any major key the 'quality' or type of each chord is as follows:

   I is _____

   II is _____

   III is_____

   IV is _____

   V is _____

   VI is _____

   VII is _____

2. The notes in the D major scale are as follows: D E F# G A B C#

   What would the 7 chords in the key of D be? (**Hint:** major, minor, minor etc)

   _____

3. Are the statements below true or false?

   In any major key triad chords I, IV and V are major.   _____

   In any major key the II, IV and VI triad chords are minor.   _____

   Chord VII is a diminished triad.   _____

   The formula major, minor, minor, major, major, minor, diminished only works for figuring out the chords in the key of C. _____

To find out how you did, check the answers on the next page!

How Did You Do?

1. *I is* **major**

   II is **minor**

   III is **minor**

   IV is **major**

   V is **major**

   VI is **minor**

   VII is **diminished**

2. *The chords in the key of D major are:*

   D major, E minor, F# minor, G major, A major, B minor, C# diminished

3. *In any major key triad chords I, IV and V are major.*
   This is true!

   In any major key the II, IV and VI triad chords are minor.
   False! Chord IV is major not minor. Chords II, III and VI are minor!

   Chord VII is a diminished triad.
   True!

   The formula major, minor, minor, major, major, minor, diminished only works for figuring out the chords in the key of C.
   False! It works for all 12 major scales to give the chords in every major key!

Chapter 7:
A Closer Look at V and VI Chords

In the last chapter we explored the chord building formula to create chord families from a major scale. We labelled each chord with a Roman numeral from I to VII.

This means we can describe a chord in a chord family with a number (e.g. 'the one chord', 'the four chord' etc) and we've seen how useful this is.

Before we look at using these different chords in common chord progressions, I want to highlight two important chords in a chord family: the '*V*' and '*VI*' chords.

The V Chord

As we saw in the last chapter, the '*V chord*' is the triad we build on the 5th note in the major scale. In the key of **C** it looks like this:

C D E **F** **G** A **B** C **D** E F G A B C

This gives us a **G** major chord made up from the notes **G**, **B** and **D**.

Grab your uke and play this G chord, noticing how you are playing those three notes:

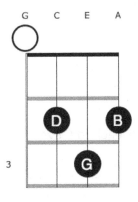

Now play **G** followed by **C**. Loop it around a few times, strumming each chord 4 times in each bar:

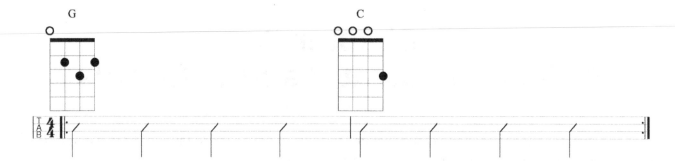

Notice the 'pull' between the two chords caused by the movement of the B note (2nd fret 1st string) to the C note (3rd fret).

This is what makes the V chord useful! It has a strong 'pull' back to the I chord. For this reason, it is often used as a way to transition to the **I** chord in a chord sequence.

The traditional name for the V chord going to the I chord is a '*perfect cadence*'. You don't need to worry about this too much, but now you know what it means if you ever hear it talked about.

But that's not all you need to know about the V chord. Sometimes we do something a little different to it...

The Dominant 7th Chord

Let's try another common **V** to **I** chord change. Play the chords below:

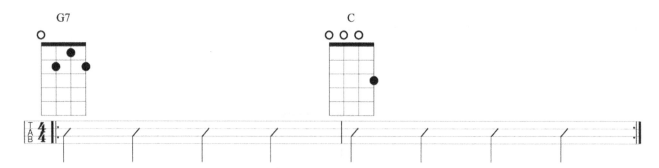

Can you hear the difference? The **G7** pulls back to **C** *even more* than the plain **G** chord did!

The introduction of the **G7** chord has *strengthened* the pull of **V** back to **I**.

So where does this G7 chord come from and does it relate back to the C major scale?

Now remember, we are in the key of C for our example here, so we would expect to be using our 7 major scale notes (C D E F G A B) and the chords in the C major chord family.

G7 contains 4 notes: **G**, **B**, **D** and **F**.

So, ask yourself this: do the notes G B D F belong in our C major scale?

Yes, they are all found in the C major scale:

C D E F **G** A **B** C **D** E **F** G A B C

We know that we can use G as the root of one of our chords because it is in the C major scale and our V chord was a G major triad.

And we know B, D and F will fit in the key because they were the notes in our B diminished triad we saw in the last chapter.

So G7 will still 'fit' with the key of C because it doesn't contain any notes which are not found in the C major scale. All we have really done is take the root of our V chord triad (G) and added the notes of our VII chord diminished triad (B, D, F) to it.

You can clearly see this in the diagrams below:

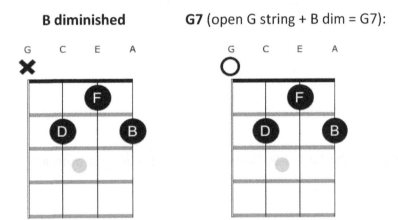

B diminished   **G7** (open G string + B dim = G7):

G7 is an example of a '***dominant 7th***' chord. Its name is actually 'G dominant 7th' although this is almost always shortened to G7 ('*G seven*').

You Might Be Wondering…

Does it matter whether we use G or G7? Are they interchangeable?

Whether you use a G or G7 as your V chord may depend on which goes best with the melody of the song you're playing or which you think sounds best!

They are basically interchangeable when we're using them as the V chord in a key.

Are Dominant 7th chords only used for the V chord in a key?

Strictly speaking, yes. But in practice, no!

Sometimes other major *or* even minor chords in a key which are *not* the V chord are changed to a dominant7 chord. Even though this technically doesn't 'fit' with the key, it can still sometimes sound good! We'll be seeing some other examples of this later in the book.

Does this work in every key?

Yes! The V chord of every key can be 'modified' to become a V7. Let's take a look.

Where you see the text '**see online video example**' below, visit **www.ukuleletheory.com** to watch a demonstration.

Play the following example in the key of F. Here we are using both C and C7 for the V chord (yes, you can use both versions if you want!). Listen to the 'pull' V has; it *really* wants to take us back to chord I *(see online video example)*:

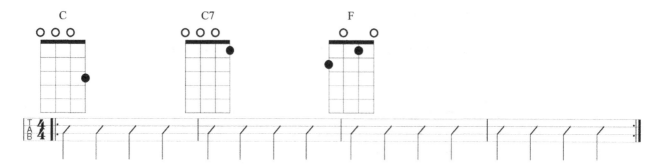

The next example is in the key of D. Here the V chord is played both as A and A7 *(see online video example)*:

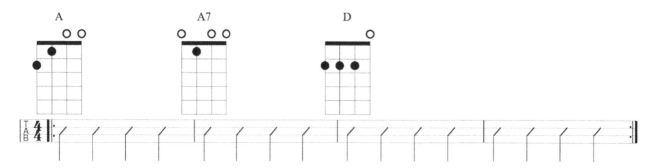

Again, we can hear how A7 (V) wants to transition back to D (V). So, you now know what a dominant7 or '7' chord is and how it's used to give the V chord in a key a strong 'pull' back to the I chord.

This simple trick gives the chord progression more motion and excitement and is a staple part of virtually *every* kind of music: so don't forget about V to I movements and '7' chords!

The VI Chord

Another important chord in any key is the '**VI chord**'. You might remember that this is a minor chord.

When played in a sequence of I-VI-IV-V it produces an instantly recognisable series of chord changes.

In fact, there is even a song about this chord sequence called '**Those Magic Changes**'.

It features in the film *Grease* and in some versions *Sha Na Na*, who recorded it, actually sing the names of the chords in the intro!

A more modern example of this chord sequence being used is in Ed Sheeran's massive hit '**Perfect**'.

Let's hear what the I-VI-IV-V chord progression sounds like.

Grab your uke and play the chords shown below to hear it in the key of C *(see online video example)*:

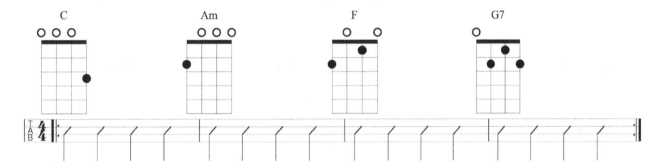

Recognise the sound?

Here it is in the key of F *(see online video example)*:

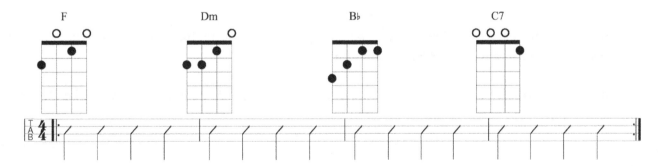

I've just given examples in two different keys here, but this sequence produces exactly the same result in *any* major key.

The 'Relative Minor'

Time for some more terminology!

The VI chord in a key is often called the *relative minor* because it is so closely related to chord I. In fact, the notes in the two chords are almost the same!

We can see this by looking at common chord shapes.

Look how similar the chord shapes for F and it's relative minor Dm are:

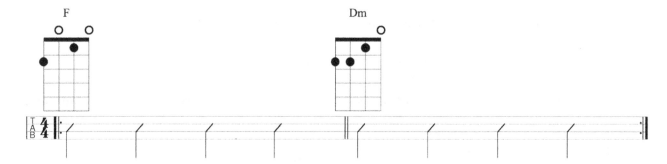

We can see this again by looking at the chord shapes for A and its relative minor chord F#m:

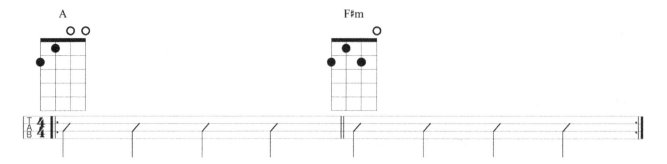

The chord change from the I chord to its relative minor (VI) is *so* common that I would really recommend you give some time to training your ear to detect it.

I think it's even worth memorising all the I-VI chord movements, at least in the common ukulele keys shown in the table in Chapter 5.

You Might Be Wondering...

Does the relative minor VI chord always follow the I chord?

No!

For instance, one of the most common chord progressions *ever* is I-V-VI-IV. This is the chord sequence that comedy band *Axis of Awesome* used in their famous YouTube sketch called '*4 Chord Song*'.

Search for it online and see these guys use the same chord sequence to play *38* hugely popular songs by a variety of music legends, from The Beatles to Lady Gaga!

Let's compare it to the I-VI-IV-V progression we covered a moment ago. Play the two examples below:

Key of C *(see online video example)*:

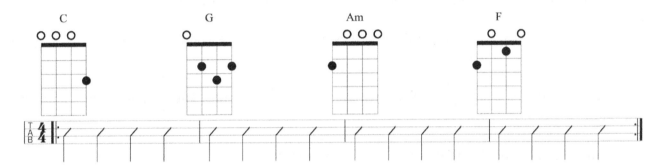

Key of F *(see online video example)*:

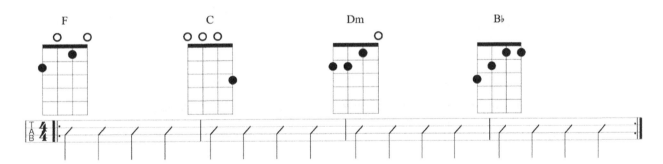

Notice how in both of these examples we're not using dominant7 chords on chord V (G and C).

This is because they tend to move better when going to chord I and here they aren't doing this, instead they're moving to chord VI (Am and Dm).

Chord VI does not always have to go after chord I, in fact any combination of I, VI , IV and V is extremely common.

And that's about all you need to know about chord V and chord VI for now. These two chords are used everywhere, so look out for them in the songs you play on your uke.

Before you move on, test yourself with the quiz that follows and check your answers to see how you did.

When you're ready I'll see you in the next chapter.

Now, Test Yourself On V And VI Chords!

1. The root of the V and V7 chords is the _____ note of the parent scale.

2. We can use two kinds of chord when playing the V chord. It can be played as a _____ or _____ chord.

3. The V7 creates a strong pull back towards the _____ chord. The proper name for this is a _____ cadence.

4. The relative minor is chord number _____ in any key.

5. Many common chord sequences use chords I, _____ , _____ and _____ from within the key (insert Roman numerals).

To find out how you did, check the answers on the next page!

How Did You Do?

1. *The root of the V and V7 chords is the **5th** note of the parent scale.*

2. *We can use two kinds of chord when playing the V chord. It can be played as a **major** or **dominant7** chord.*

3. *The V7 creates a strong pull back towards the **I** chord. The proper name for this is a **perfect cadence**.*

4. *The relative minor is chord number **VI** in any key.*

5. *Many common chord sequences use chords I, **VI, IV** and **V** from within the key (in various orders and combinations).*

Chapter 8:
Chord Progressions and
'The Roman Numeral Short-Cut'

Ok, it's time to start putting our new knowledge into practice!

We know how to make chord families in our major keys and how to identify each chord in a family with a Roman numeral. The Roman numeral is based on the position of a chord's root note in the major scale.

For example, in the key of C:

F major is the **IV** chord. This is because it is the triad built on the **4th** note in the C major scale.

We have seen that it's possible to build **7 chords** from our major scale giving a series of major and minor chords and one diminished chord:

I	II	III	IV	V	VI	VII
MAJOR	MINOR	MINOR	MAJOR	MAJOR	MINOR	DIMINISHED

Here is a reminder of what this looks like when we apply it to the **C** major scale to get the chord family for the key of **C** major:

I	II	III	IV	V	VI	VII
C	Dm	Em	F	G	Am	Bdim

In this chapter we're going to look at putting these chords into different sequences or '*chord progressions*' to form the basis for a song or piece of music.

Some of the more complex examples coming up have video demonstrations which you can find online at **www.ukuleletheory.com** - so look out for those.

Note: For now, we'll ignore the diminished chord (chord VII), simply because it is so rarely played in most music. The fact is, you'll probably only use chords I-VI in a key.

Common Chord Progression 1: I-IV-V

Grab your uke and play this common chord progression in the key of **C** *(see online video example)*:

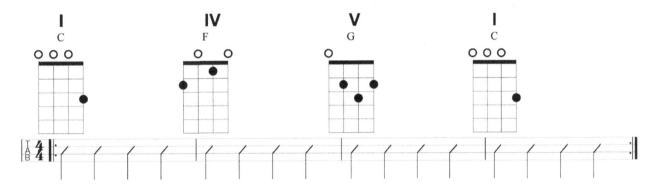

Look at the Roman numerals written above the chord shapes and you'll see that this is a simple I-IV-V chord progression. Check they're the right chords using the table we just looked at.

Don't like it in C? Ok, let's try it in the key of **G**. Here is the **G** major chord family:

I	II	III	IV	V	VI	VII
G	Am	Bm	C	D	Em	F#dim

Can you spot what chords you'd play for a I-IV-V chord progression in the key of G?

When you've worked it out check your answer and hear what it sounds like by playing the following example *(see online video example)*:

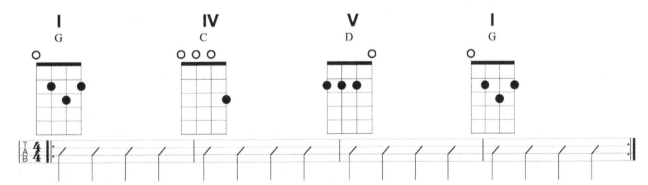

The I-IV-V chord progression is probably the most common sequence of chords ever invented! To hear a really famous song using it listen to *'La Bamba'*!

Now have a go at building some I-IV-V progressions on your own: choose a key, find the I IV and V chords from the table of chord families in Appendix 1 and go for it!

Work with this I-IV-V idea until it really makes sense to you, when it does the rest of this section is going to be easy

Common Chord Progression 2: I-VI-IV-V

Let's look at another progression this time using chord VI, the relative minor we talked about in the last chapter.

Grab your uke and play this one in the key of **C** *(see online video example)*:

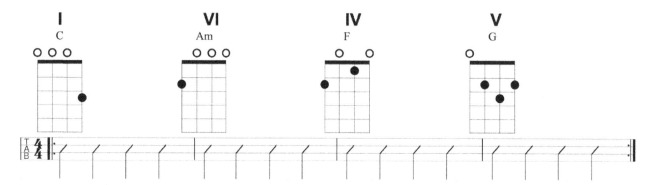

The Roman numerals written above the chord shapes tell you this is a I-VI-IV-V chord progression. Check they're the right chords using the **C** major chord family table a few pages back.

Let's move this into another key now: the key of **F**. First, play it on your uke *(see online video example)*:

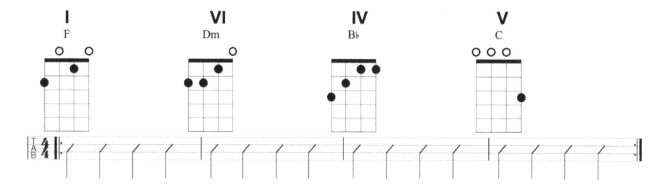

Look at the **F** major chord family and you can clearly see why this is a I-VI-IV-V chord progression:

I	II	III	IV	V	VI	VII
F	Gm	Am	Bb	C	Dm	Edim

Common Chord Progression 3: I-V-VI-IV

Let's try one more: here is a I-V-VI-IV chord progression in the key of **C** *(see online video example)*:

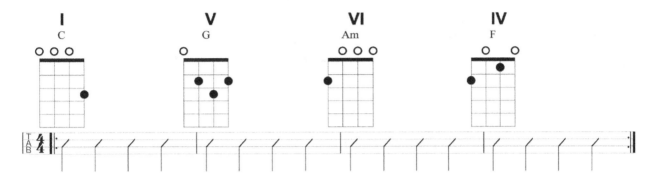

I'm sure you're probably getting the hang of how this works now, but here it is in the key of **G**. Check the chords in the **G** major chord family table a few pages ago to help this make total sense, then play it on your uke to hear how it sounds *(see online video example)*:

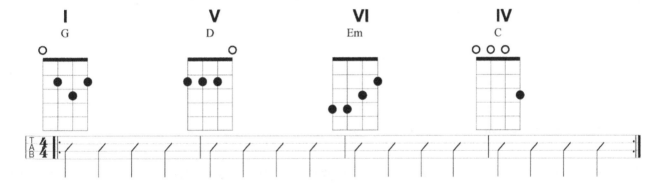

Adding the II and III Chords

We haven't used a II or III chord yet, but this doesn't mean they are not used: they are!

Let's be a bit more ambitious and use more of the chords in our chord family.

This example should do the trick; it's in the key of **F** and uses all of chords I to VI.

Play it and listen to how the different chord changes affect the 'feel' or 'mood' of the chord progression *(see online video example)*:

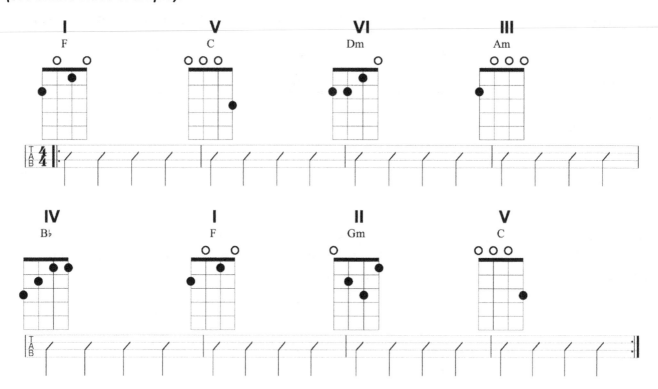

Can you hear the more 'wistful' mood created by putting more minor chords into this progression?

It's similar to the chord progression you'd use to play a song like *'Streets of London'*.

One more thing on this chord progression...

Think back to the last chapter and you'll hopefully remember that:

The V chord in a key can be played as major (V major) *or* as a dominant 7th chord (V7) depending on the sound that will suit the song we're playing

Let's take the last example and extend it to get a longer chord progression.

I'm also going to add in some V7 chords.

Play the following example to hear the difference doing this makes to the progression, then I'll explain why I play it this way *(see online video example)*:

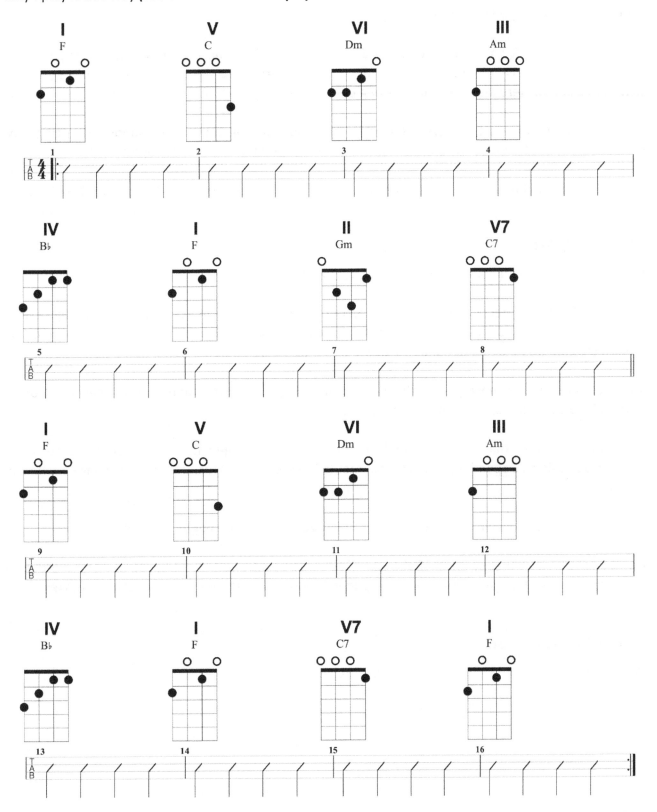

In this chord progression, **C** or **C7** can be used to play the **V** chord.

Which one to use depends on *where it is going next*.

When V is going to F, I am playing C7 (bars 8-9 and 15-16). This is because F is chord I and you might remember that V7 gives us a strong 'pull' back to the I chord. I like the sound of this 'pull' and this is why I am using C7 here instead of just playing C.

When chord V is going to Dm (bars 2-3 and 10-11) I'm just playing C. I think it sounds better that way. C7 'pulls' to F, but that's not where we want to go at this point in the chord progression!

Of course, you might want to do it differently so feel free to experiment with the different options.

Summing Up...

Let's consider the main points we can take away from this chapter:

Firstly, the Roman numeral chord numbering system gives us a 'short cut' for playing chord progressions in different keys. By working out the numbers of the chords in a progression, we can use them to find out which chords to play if we want to move it into a new key.

The musical term for moving something into a new key is 'transposition'. So, we can use Roman numerals to easily *transpose* a chord progression.

Secondly, we can see that our chord family members can be arranged in different sequences to create chord progressions. Depending on how we combine the possible chords, the result will have a different 'mood' or 'feel'.

I hope you can see how we are putting everything together now and beginning to make music!

Don't be in a hurry with any of this. Take your time and go back over anything you need to in order for it to make sense. Then you'll have a perfect understanding of all the wonderful stuff that makes music work!

It's time for another test...

Now, Test Yourself On Chord Sequences!

1. Using the chord / key chart in Appendix 1 to help, write out a I IV V chord sequence in the given keys:

   Key of G: _____

   Key of F: _____

   Key of A: _____

2. Using the chord / key chart to help, write out a I VI II V chord sequence in the given keys:

   Key of D: _____

   Key of G: _____

   Key of A: _____

3. Add Roman numerals to the chords below to describe the chord sequence in the given keys:

   Key of **G**:

   # | G / / / | C / / / | Bm / / / | Am / D / |

   ___   ___   ___   ___ ___

   Key of **C**:

   # | C / / / | Am / / / | Dm / / / | G7 / / / |

   ___   ___   ___   ___

To find out how you did, check the answers on the next page!

How Did You Do?

1. *I IV V in key of G:* **G C D**

   I IV V in key of F: **F Bb C**

   I IV V in key of A: **A D E**

   (Any V chord could also be played as a V7!)

2. *I VI II V in key of D:* **D Bm Em A**

   I VI II V in key of G: **G Em Am D**

   I VI II V in key of A: **A F#m Bm E**

   (Any V chord could also be played as a V7!)

3. Add Roman numerals the chords below to describe the chord sequence in the given keys:

   Key of **G**:

   | G / / / | C / / / | Bm / / / | Am / D / |
     I   IV   III   II   V

   Key of **C**:

   | C / / / | Am / / / | Dm / / / | G7 / / / |
     I   VI   II   V

Chapter 9:
Chord Progressions with 'Stand-In Chords'

In the last chapter we looked at some examples of progressions which used the chords contained within a particular chord family. Lots of the time chord progressions and songs only use the chords found in their chord family, but there are some big exceptions to this!

You might remember that back in Chapter 5 we asked: 'Can you use a chord from *outside* the chord family of a particular key?'

We said that yes, sometimes we can.

It is actually quite common to see a 'foreign' chord in a chord progression. By this I mean a chord which is **not** found in the chord family that goes with the key you're in.

I want to make sure that we cover this so that when you see it happening in any music you play, it isn't confusing or off-putting.

'Stand-In Chords'

Often when we see a 'foreign' chord in a progression it is acting as a replacement or '*stand-in*' for the normal chord we'd expect to see from the chord family.

Let's look at a quick example. Play this I-VI-II-V chord progression in the key of C *(see online video example)*:

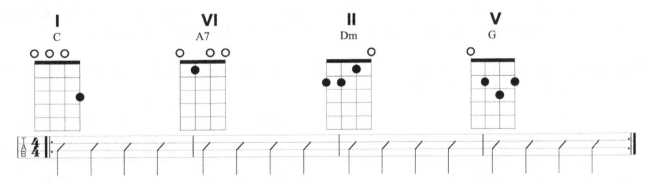

Notice anything strange?

That's right: sticking to our C major chord family, chord VI *should* be A minor, but it's not! Instead we're playing an A7 chord. The A7 is acting as a 'stand-in chord' for A minor.

You can hopefully hear how the chord sequence still works despite this chord being changed, perhaps you think it actually sounds better!

You see, here's the thing: even though we've broken the 'rules' by doing this, sometimes *breaking* the rules can create some great sounding music!

Let's look at this 'stand-in' concept and play some examples which use it.

To keep things simple, I'm going to use the term '***stand-in chord***' for any chord we use in a progression which is outside the chord family. There are more musically correct names I could use, but 'stand-in chord' describes what's really going on here, so that is the name we'll use for the time being.

What Are The Common 'Stand-In Chords'?

The good news is that there is an easy way to learn about *stand-in chords* and play them in all sorts of keys just using the information you already have.

You see:

> *Most of the time, stand-in chords are simply one of the minor chords in the key,*
> *changed into a major or dominant7 chord*

Let's look at this more closely. Here is our chord family in the key of C:

I	II	III	IV	V	VI	VII
C	Dm	Em	F	G	Am	Bdim

Now we just said that most stand-in chords are simply chords II, III or VI in the key changed into **major** or **7**. The diminished chord (VII) is sometimes changed in this way too, as we'll soon see.

This gives us a '***modified***' chord family which we could use as well. It contains some useful chords which could stand in for chords II, III, VI and VII:

I	II	III	IV	V	VI	VII
C	D/D7	E/E7	F	G	A/A7	B/B7

Just to be clear, we are 'twisting' the key of C chord family here. I'm not saying these chords belong in the chord family ...strictly speaking they don't!

We are *modifying* or *altering* the chord family to get some other sounds which can work as well. Don't worry, this modification is not random, there are very good reasons why it works! The most important thing is that changing these chords can sound *great*, as you'll hear for yourself in a moment.

Stand-In Chord Progression 1:

Now grab your uke and play this *(see online video example)*:

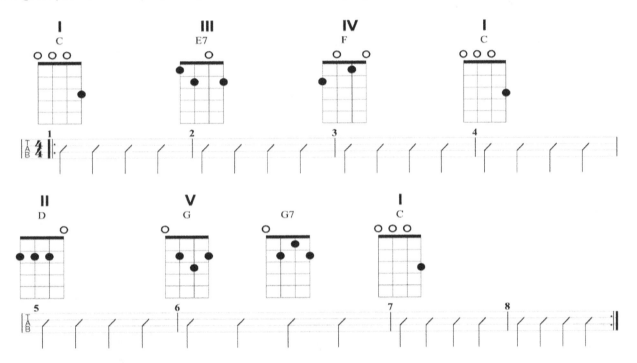

Now there's a lot going on in this simple progression:

C, F, G and **G7** are acting normally as **I, IV** and **V** chords in the key of **C**.

The **E7** chord in **bar 2** is a 'stand-in' chord for the normal **III** chord: **Em**.

Look at how the notes along the 4th string are moving as you go from C to E7 to F. See how they are 'climbing up' in semitones?

This creates tension, pulling you up towards the F chord in a really strong sounding way. That is why the E7 sounds so good as a 'stand-in' here!

In **bar 5**, D stands in for the usual II chord: Dm. This also means that the C chord in the previous bar is moving up **one tone** or a **whole-step** to the D chord. I call this 'the whole-step up' movement. This is very common and is usually followed by the normal V chord of the key in which we are playing.

In **bars 5-6** D goes to G (chord V as expected!). Notice something here? D is the *V chord of G* so it naturally has that 'pull' towards G that we talked about earlier.

Finally, in **bars 6-7** G goes back to C. This is the normal V chord (with a bit of help from G7) 'going home' to C (our I chord).

So, even though there is lots going on there, you can see that really all that has happened is that some of the chords which would *normally* be played as minor have been changed into major or dominant7 chords. Listen to the difference it makes: the chord sequence has a whole new sound!

Stand-In Chord Progression 2:

Now look at this one from the key of **C** with 'stand-in' chords *(see online video example)*:

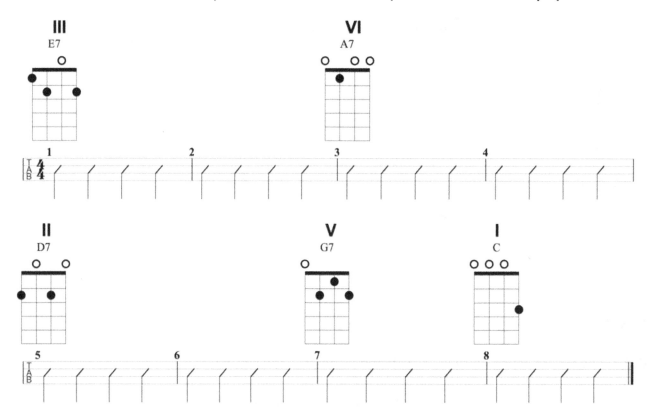

You can see how chords **III**, **VI** and **II** have *all* been changed from minor chords into dominant7 chords. But there is something else at work here too! Each of the dominant7 chords in the sequence is moving to the chord that would *normally* be its I chord.

Let's take a look at this:

Bars 1-3: E7 is *standing in* for Em. But it is *also* the V chord of A7, the next chord in the sequence. So, it is 'pulling' us towards the A7 in bar 3.

Bars 3-5: A7 is *standing in* for Am. But it is *also* the V chord of D7, the next chord in the sequence. So, it is 'pulling' us towards the D7 in bar 5.

Bars 5-7: D7 is *standing in* for Dm. But it is *also* the V chord of G7, the next chord in the sequence. So, it is 'pulling' us towards the G7 in bar 7.

Bars 7-8: G7 is the V chord of C, the next chord in the sequence. It is used to pull us back to our I chord.

Make sense? Here are a couple more examples to try. Can you analyse these yourself using what you now know?

Exercise 1 *(see online video example)*:

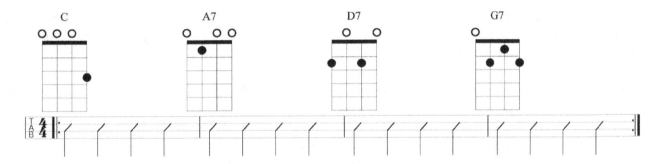

(**Answer**: Chords VI and II (Am and Dm) have been changed to dominant7 chords (A7 and D7)

Exercise 2 *(see online video example)*:

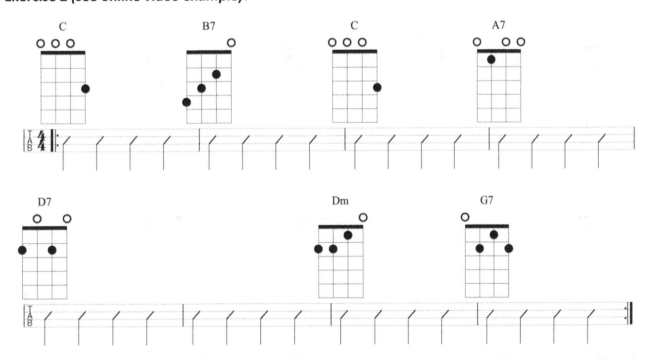

It's trickier this one, can you see what's happening?

(**Answer**: Chord VII has been changed here! Instead of B diminished it has become B7. Chord VI is A7 instead of Am. D7 stands in for Dm …but then it changes back to Dm again. Finally, G7 acts as V to go back to I at the start when it repeats).

And That's It On 'Stand-In Chords' For Now …

Hopefully you can now spot a 'stand-in chord' in a chord progression and have some idea of what it's doing there! Before we leave this topic…

If I could stress one thing at this point, it's to **listen to the sound** of these chord movements and get familiar with them. Also, listen out for them (or maybe parts of them) in any songs you play and see if you can spot them in song books or song sheets you use (they'll be in there for sure!).

You may well recognise them in songs which are popular to play on the uke; songs like '*You're Sixteen*', '*Who's Sorry Now?*', '*A Fool Such As I*' (Elvis' version), '*What A Day For A Daydream*' and '*Ain't No Pleasing You*' (Chas and Dave).

There are many other possible ways to use these stand-in chords with our normal chord families, but we can't cover them all, there are simply too many to show here!

Play around with these ideas in different keys too, perhaps start by moving the examples we've seen here into some familiar ukulele keys. Use the table in Appendix 1 to help with this.

In the meantime, here's a great one to doodle with! It's shown in the key of **F**. Play it any way you like, change the key, just have fun with it *(see online video example)*. Enjoy!

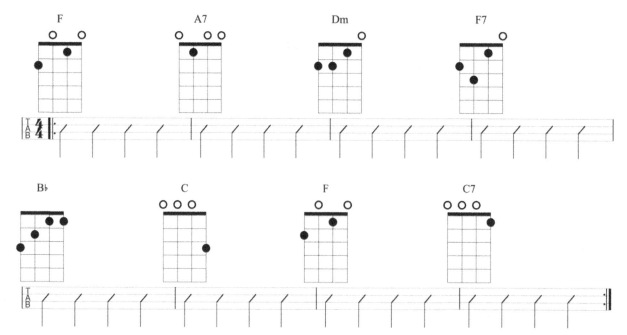

Hint: notice the I chord briefly becomes a dominant7 chord in this one!

Now, Test Yourself On Stand-In Chords!

1. Which type of chord is most often used as a stand-in chord? _____

2. Which number chords in the chord family are most commonly replaced by a stand-in chord?

   _____

3. In the chord sequence E7 – A7 – D7 – G7 – C each of the dominant7 chords is moving to its

   own _____ chord.

4. Take a look at this I, VI, II, V chord sequence in G and re-write it using stand-ins for chords for

   VI and II:

G | Em | Am | D7

   _____

To find out how you did, check the answers on the next page!

How Did You Do?

1. *The most common kind of chord to use as a stand-in is a **dominant7 chord.***

2. ***Chords II, III, VI and VII** are most commonly replaced by a stand-in chord (normally a dominant7 chord)*

3. *In the chord sequence E7 – A7 – D7 – G7 – C each of the dominant7 chords is moving to its own **I** chord.*

4. *Using stand-in chords for VI and II, the chord sequence looks like this:*

G | E7 | A7 | D7

Chapter 10:
Minor Keys

By now you should have a really good grasp of major keys and their chord families. This will help you make sense of so many songs you might go on to learn on your uke.

But not *all* music is in a major key, some songs are in what is called a '*minor key*'.

For this reason, we're going to take a quick look at minor keys now.

Once again in this chapter, some of the more complex examples have video demonstrations. Find them online at **www.ukuleletheory.com**

Minor Keys And Major Keys: What's The Difference?

The main difference is in the way they *sound*, so comparing the sound of a major and a minor key is a great place to start.

Play the following chord progression in the key of D major *(see online video example)*:

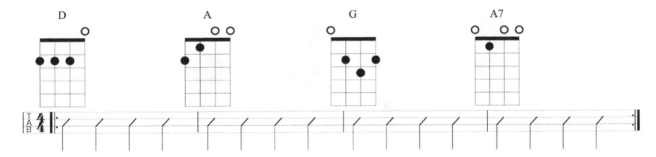

Next, play the following chord progression in the key of D minor *(see online video example)*:

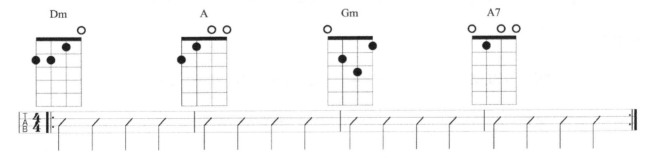

Notice the difference?

The minor key sequence has a sadder, sombre sound or mood. In contrast, the major key sequence creates a brighter, happier sound. Composers will choose to use a major or minor key depending on the mood or effect they want the music to have on the listener.

In a previous chapter we built major keys and major chord families using the notes in the major scale.

We do exactly the same thing to get minor keys and minor chord families, the difference is that instead of using the major scale as our parent scale, we use the '*natural minor scale*'.

The Natural Minor Scale: What You Need To Know

Like the major scale, the '*natural minor scale*' is a scale made up of **7** notes.

Let's compare the two scales side by side:

C major scale: C D E F G A B C

C natural minor: C D **Eb** F G **Ab Bb** C

Although some notes are in both scales, you can see that the 3rd, 6th and 7th notes are different. They have been flattened in the natural minor scale.

Here's a scale pattern for the C natural minor scale on the uke. Play it and listen to how it sounds:

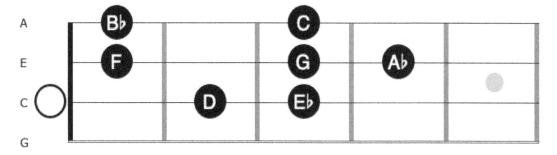

As you can hear, it sounds quite different to the major scale. Both the notes in the scale and the sound it makes are different because the *tone / semitone* formula of the scale is different.

It's this:

TONE – SEMITONE – TONE – TONE – SEMITONE – TONE – TONE

Compare it to the major scale formula we saw earlier to see how it differs.

Now, when we follow this sequence from any starting note we get a natural minor scale beginning on whatever note we started the formula on.

So that's your crash course on the natural minor scale. You may not ever need to play this, but some knowledge of it is useful because we'll be using it as our parent scale to create minor keys.

Let's move on...

Building Minor Key Chord Families

Remember how we built a triad on each note of the major scale to get major key chord families?

Well the good news is that the process for building minor chord families is exactly the same! The only difference is that we apply it to the *natural minor scale*.

Now, don't get worried about this, you're not going to have to learn a whole lot of new chords!

Most of the chords you'll actually use to play in the 'uke friendly' minor keys you'll easily recognise as soon as you see them.

I'm not actually going to take you through the whole process of building triads on each note of the scale like we did to the major scale ...

Instead, there's a really handy 'shortcut' for taking everything you know about major keys and using it to instantly learn your minor keys!

The 'Relative Minor Shortcut'

Our old friend, the relative minor gives us a fantastic shortcut when it comes to working out minor key chord families.

Remember how the relative minor chord is built on the **6th** note of the major scale? It's chord VI in any major key chord family.

You can see from the C major chord family below that the relative minor of C is Am:

I	II	III	IV	V	VI	VII
C	Dm	Em	F	G	Am	Bdim

Here comes the *shortcut* I promised ...

Simply rearrange the chords starting on the **Am** chord instead of C.

So Am becomes our new 'I chord':

I	II	III	IV	V	VI	VII
Am	Bdim	C	Dm	Em	F	G

We now have the chords in the key of **A** minor. Notice how the major chord we started with, **C**, has now become the **III** chord in the minor sequence.

Now, Test Yourself!

Here are the chords in the key of **F** major:

I	II	III	IV	V	VI	VII
F	Gm	Am	B♭	C	Dm	Edim

The relative minor is **Dm**.

Using the relative minor shortcut, write the chords in the key of Dm into the table below:

I	II	III	IV	V	VI	VII

Answers: Dm (I), Edim (II), F (III), Gm (IV), Am (V), Bb (VI), C (VII)

'Uke Friendly' Minor Keys

Due to the nature of the ukulele, certain minor keys are much easier to use than others. For this reason, they are the ones you are most likely to encounter.

The table below shows the chord families for these 'uke friendly' minor keys, choose a key and experiment with the chords in the chord family (just ignore all the diminished chords for now!):

KEY	I	II	III	IV	V	VI	VII
Am	Am	Bdim	C	Dm	Em	F	G
Em	Em	F#dim	G	Am	Bm	C	D
Dm	Dm	Edim	F	Gm	Am	B*b*	C
Bm	Bm	C#dim	D	Em	F#m	G	A

(**Note**: for your information a complete table of minor chord families can be found at the back of the book).

You Might Be Wondering...

If the chords in a major key and the corresponding relative minor key are all the same then what's the difference? Why don't chord sequences sound the same?

It's all to do with what the ear hears as the main chord.

In a C major chord progression, the C chord would be 'framed' so that we hear it as the 'home' or main chord.

In an A minor chord progression, we might be using the same chords, but the Am would be 'framed' as the main chord. Very often (but not always) the first chord in the progression will 'set the mood'.

Play the next example in the key of Dm.

Even though the chords are also in the key of F major, our ear 'hears' Dm as the I chord or 'home' chord *(see online video example)*:

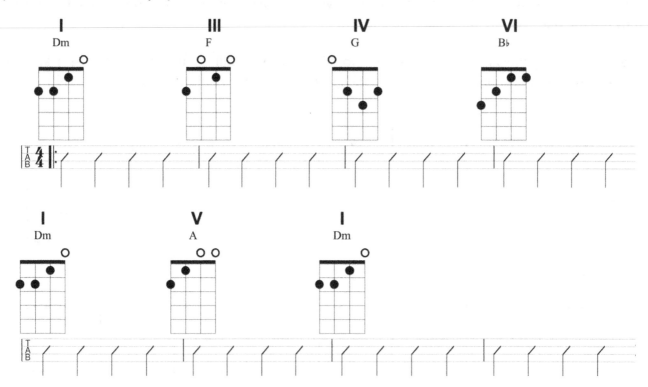

I'm sure that sounds familiar, doesn't it? You can hear how, even though Dm is the only minor chord in the progression, it's 'framed' in such a way to create the 'sadder' minor key sound.

Common Chord Progressions And 'Stand-In Chords'

Look at the chords for **Dm** chord family in the table and then look at the chord progression you just played again. The **F** and **B♭** chords are in the chord family, but the **G** and **A** are not. These are 'stand-ins' for **Gm** (IV) and Am (V).

It is extremely common to use stand-in chords in minor keys, they add tension and colour and stop things sounding too sad or sombre!

The most popular chord to replace in a minor key is the V chord. Instead of minor, we often replace it with a major or dominant7 chord. This gives us that useful 'pull' back to the I chord, just like it does in a major key.

Play the following chord progression in D minor and hear how the standard V chord (Am) has been replaced by A and A7.

Notice how strongly the A7 'pulls' us back to Dm! *(see online video example)*:

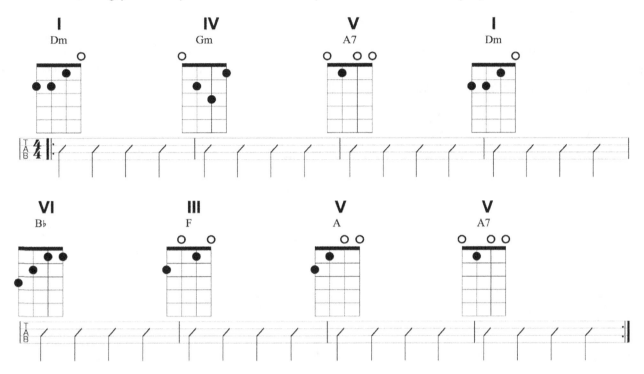

This next example is in the key of Em. It reminds me of '*Let Her Go*' by Passenger. I recommend you listen to it, it's a great example of a well-known song in a minor key.

Notice how here the V chord has not been changed; it is the standard Bm chord in the E minor chord family *(see online video example)*:

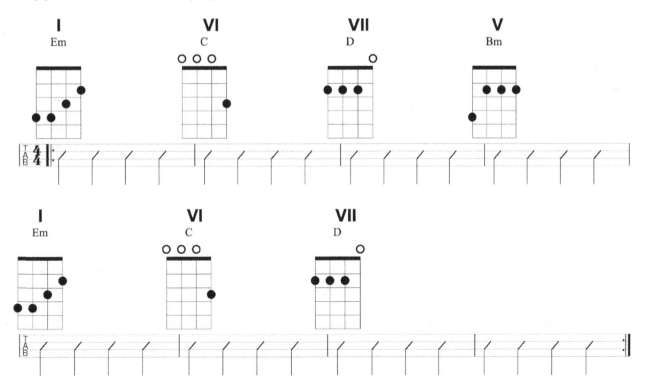

Our final example is in the key of **A minor**. Here, **E7** is replacing **Em** as the **V** chord at the end of the progression.

It's also using C 'major 7' (written Cmaj7) in place of the standard C chord. We'll be looking at 'maj7' chords in the next chapter. You might recognise this chord progression; it's similar to the disco classic *'I Will Survive' (see online video example)*:

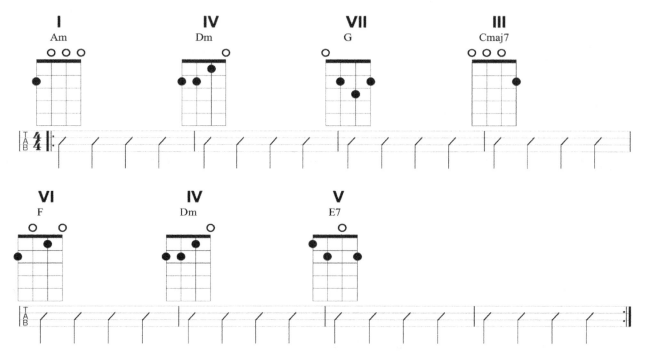

So now you know most of what you need to know about minor keys.

We've seen how:

- We use the *natural minor scale* to build chord families for minor keys.
- We can use the 'relative minor shortcut' to convert our major chord families into minor chord families (remember this useful trick!).
- Major or dominant7 chords are often used as 'stand-ins' in minor key chord progressions, especially chords IV and V. They will often make minor chord progressions stronger and more appealing. In case you're wondering, there is a music theory 'reason' for why this works ...but we don't need to worry about this for now!

So that's the fundamental first steps to understanding minor keys. There are things about minor keys we *haven't* covered here, but this chapter gives you all the most important things you need to know.

In the next chapter we are going to wrap up our music theory journey by looking at a few loose ends. These are based on some of the most common questions that I get asked by my ukulele students.

So, test yourself on minor keys with the questions coming up next, check your answers and I'll see you in the final chapter!

Now, Test Yourself On Minor Keys...

1. The natural minor scale contains _____ notes.

2. To change a major scale to a natural minor scale we have to flatten _____ notes: the 3rd, _____ and _____ notes.

3. We can use the VI chord or _____ of a major chord family to create a minor chord family.

4. Here are the chords in the G major chord family:

I	II	III	IV	V	VI	VII
G	Am	Bm	C	D	Em	F#dim

Using the following table, fill in the chord family for the key of E minor:

I	II	III	IV	V	VI	VII

5. In a minor key, chords IV and V are minor but 'stand-in chords' are often used to make stronger sounding chord progressions. Fill in the common 'stand-in' guidelines below:

IV is often changed from minor to _____.

V is often changed from minor to _____ or _____.

To find out how you did, check the answers on the next page!

How Did You Do?

1. The natural minor scale contains **7** notes.

2. To change a major scale to a natural minor scale we have to flatten **3** notes: the 3rd, **6th** and **7th** notes.

3. We can use the VI chord or **relative minor** of a major chord family to create a minor chord family.

4. The chord family for the key of E minor is:

I	II	III	IV	V	VI	VII
Em	F#dim	G	Am	Bm	C	D

5. Common 'stand-in chords' in minor keys:

   IV is often changed from minor to **major**.

   V is often changed from minor to **major** or **dominant7 (7).**

Chapter 11:
Loose Ends

We have covered a lot so far in this introduction to music theory. In fact, you now know most of what you will probably ever need to know as a uke player!

In this chapter I just want to discuss a few 'loose ends'. These are things you'll probably come across and which often prompt questions from students.

Let's go through them one at a time.

Don't forget to watch the video examples at **www.ukuleletheory.com**

Dominant7 'Joining Chords'

I'm often asked why we sometimes see the I chord in a key played as a dominant7 chord as shown in the following chord progression *(see online video example)*:

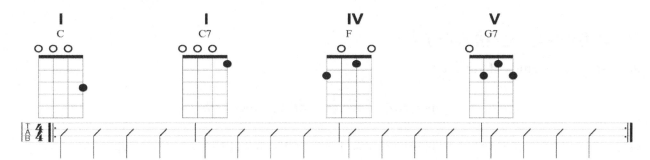

The G7 at the end makes sense; it is the V chord in the key. It's there to 'pull' you back to C again when you repeat the chord progression.

But what about the C7 in bar 2, what's that doing there?

Here's a useful tip:

> *Whenever you see an unexpected dominant7 chord in a song, always look where it is going next. This will normally help to explain why it's there*

So, look where the C7 is going; it's going to F. Is there any connection between C7 and F?

Yes! The C7 chord is the V7 chord of the F chord family so it gives us that 'pull' back to F that we talked about. So here the C7 is being used as a 'joining chord' to lead us smoothly from C to F. Even though we're actually in the key of C, the 'pull' from C7 to F still comes in handy when we need it.

If we wanted to, we could describe this as 'I7': the I chord changed to a dominant7 chord.

Here's the same thing happening in the key of **G**. See if you can spot why the G7 fits so well, you'll find the answer below *(see online video example)*:

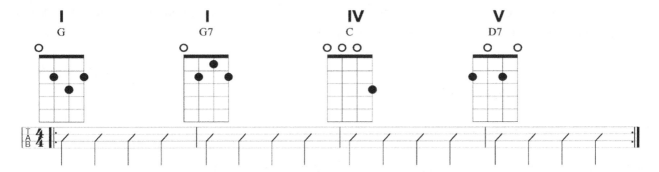

(**Answer:** G7 fits because it is the V chord of C! We are using it as a '*joining chord*' to get smoothly to C).

This little trick is everywhere in uke song books. Now, the next time you see it you'll be able to understand what's actually happening!

Other Kinds Of 7th Chord

There are 3 main kinds of 7th chord:

major 7th, minor 7th and *dominant7th*

We've seen the 'dominant7' chord already, now it's time to look at the other two types.

A word of warning: *don't* get them mixed up. These chords all contain a '7' in their name, but they are not the same thing!

The 'Major 7th' Chord

'Major 7th' chords are quite common, especially in slightly jazzy arrangements of songs.

You'll normally see them written as '*maj7*', for example '*Gmaj7*'.

I like to think of them as a 'decorated' version of a major chord. For example, CMaj7 is really just a 'decorated' C major chord.

The most common use of a major7 chord is as chord I or chord IV in a key. You wouldn't play a major7 for the V chord, that needs to be played as a dominant7 chord remember!

Major 7th chords add the 7th of the major scale to our basic major triad:

C major scale: C D E F G A B C

C triad: C E G (**root + 3rd + 5th** notes from the scale)

Cmaj7: C E G **B** (**root + 3rd + 5th + 7th** notes from the scale)

Play the chord boxes below to compare **C**, **Cmaj7** and **C7**:

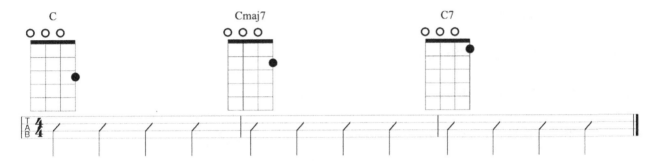

Can you see the descending note on the 1st string? It's moving from the 3rd fret, to the 2nd fret, then down to the 1st fret. This is the root (C) moving down to become the 7th (B), changing the chord from C to Cmaj7.

This then moves down to the 1st fret. This changes the 7th (B) into a flattened 7th (B*b*). This changes the chord from Cmaj7 into C7.

Here's the same thing happening to a G chord. This time you can see the moving note is on the 2nd string:

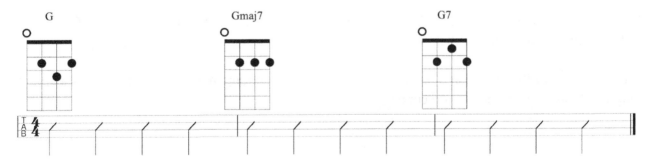

See if you can change any other major chords you know into major7 chords, it works for any of them.

Find your root, move it down a semitone and you've got a major7 chord.

The 'Minor 7th' Chord

These chords have a 'softer' sound to a regular minor chord and are written '*m7*' (e.g. Dm7, Fm7, Am7 etc).

To be honest, some minor 7 shapes are better than others on the ukulele and often in a song a regular minor chord will work just as well as a m7 chord.

Think of them as a 'decorated' version of a minor chord. For example, Em7 is really just a 'decorated' E minor chord. They are most commonly used as replacements for minor II, III and VI chords in a key.

They are formed by adding the 7th note of the natural minor scale to a normal minor chord:

A natural minor scale: A B C D E F G

Am triad: A C E (**root + 3rd + 5th** notes from the scale)

Am7: A C E **G** (**root + 3rd + 5th + 7th** notes from the scale)

Here's Am changing to Am7, play them and hear the difference in sound:

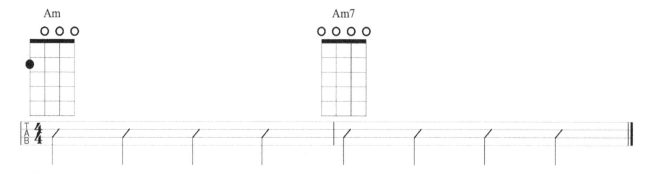

It looks as though we've removed a note here, not added one!

But look again: the top 3 notes in the chord are identical, but the Am7 chord contains a G, played by adding in the open G string (4th string).

Listen as you play the chords and particularly notice the descending note on string 4. This is a common sound in a minor to minor 7 chord change.

'Suspended Chords'

What are 'sus4' chords?

I get asked this a lot, but it's actually very simple!

In a *'sus4'* chord the 4th note in the scale replaces the 3rd in the triad.

For example:

G major scale: G A B C D E F#

G major: G B D (**root + 3rd + 5th**)

G sus4: G **C** D (**root + 4th + 5th**)

You see, 'sus' is short for 'suspended' and in a 'sus' chord we are simply 'suspending' (removing) the 3rd and replacing it with the 4th note instead.

Why bother?

It produces some beautiful musical tension, that's why!

In most cases the 'sus4' chord will return to the plain major chord. This 'resolves' the tension created by the sus4 chord. Play the example below to hear this; I'm sure you'll recognise the sound *(see online video example)*:

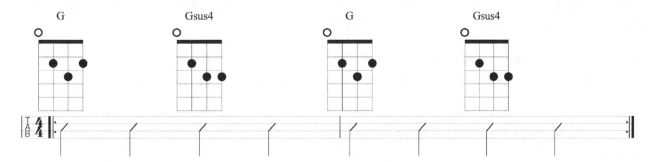

(**Tip**: leave the G chord in place when playing Gsus4. Simply use your 4th finger to play the 3rd fret on the 1st string to the G chord shape. This makes it easy to switch between them.)

What are 'sus2' chords?

The 'sus2' is exactly the same in principle but it's the 2nd note that replaces the 3rd of the triad.

C major scale: C D E F G A B C

C triad: C E G (**root + 3rd + 5th** notes from the scale)

C sus2: C **D** G (**root + 2nd + 5th** notes from the scale)

'Sus2' chords are not quite as common as sus4 chords but you will come across them.

Play this to hear a Dsus2 chord in use *(see online video example)*:

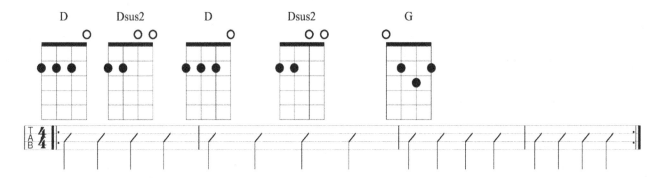

Both sus2 and sus4 chords can work nicely as the I or V chord in a key. Sometimes they'll work well on chord IV as well.

As you play around on your uke, experiment a little with sus2 and sus4 chords …they can make some great sounds!

Other Chords

There are lots of other chords you might encounter as a uke player, especially if you play any jazz or 'jazzy' versions of various songs. The names of some of these chords might look a bit intimidating, but often the chord is basically what it says on the tin!

Take a Bmin7b5 chord for example. It may sound a bit frightening, but it's just what it says: a Bmin 7 chord, formed as we saw earlier, with the 5th note of the Bmin scale (F#) flattened to become F.

Compare the chords below. The 5th of the Bm7 is on the 2nd string at the 2nd fret. Flatten it by moving it down to the 1st fret and it becomes a flattened 5th, transforming the chord into 'B minor 7th flat five' (Bm7b5):

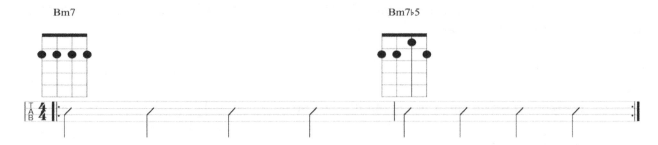

Don't worry too much about this kind of thing: it's pretty rare that you'll encounter chords like this in most of the music we play on the uke.

The purpose of this is just to show you how the name of a chord gives us 'clues' about how to play it.

Then at least if you do run into some of these weird sounding chords, you will be able to understand what the name of the chord means and maybe work out a shape to use for playing it!

You've Reached The End Of Music Theory For Ukulele!

Congratulations on reaching the end of this book!

I hope you've enjoyed your journey of discovery with me and that I've been able to clear up any confusion you may have had before you started reading this book. Hopefully you now feel like the basics of music are easier to understand than most people think!

Music theory is a vast and complex subject and we've only really dipped our toes in the water, but all the subjects we have covered *will* help you make more sense of most of the music you'll probably ever want to play.

Go over any lessons in this book again as many times as you need to, play the examples given ...and be patient, everything will eventually fall into place for you.

Above all: *listen* to the sounds the concepts we've studied give you and try to *observe* them happening in the music you play.

By analysing chord sequences in your songbooks or song sheets you can see these ideas at work ...they're all in there somewhere! Do this and you'll soon experience those 'light-bulb' moments where everything just suddenly clicks.

I get them all the time, as a musician you never stop learning!

Finally, if you can spare a few minutes, would you mind leaving me a review on this book on the platform you bought it from? I'd really appreciate it!

Thanks for reading, good luck and happy playing.

David Shipway

P.S If you're looking to expand your uke playing even further, check out my second book, '**Next Level Ukulele**', on the next page.

Also by David Shipway

If you've enjoyed this book, then check out my second book '**Next Level Ukulele**'.

It's just what you need if you want to boost your confidence when performing, develop your music theory knowledge, your rhythm and listening skills, improve your ability to play and remember songs, and transform your all-round skills as a musician.

This easy-to-use, play-along guide to understanding music, building confidence and learning to jam like a pro, ***with over 100 audio play-along practice tracks*** shows you how!

Discover how to:

- learn to play 'by ear'
- recognise major and minor chords, rhythms and time signatures, 'seventh' chords, common chord sequences, song forms and more
- nail common rhythmic styles and strumming patterns better than ever before
- massively expand your chord shape knowledge with 'moveable' chord shapes
- ...and more

This book comes with ***over 100 audio tracks*** to play along with (one of the best practice methods you can possibly use!).

You'll find it in various formats on Amazon and as an ebook on Kobo, Apple, Google Play, Barnes & Noble and other online stores.

Appendix 1:
The Complete Chord / Key Chart

This table shows you all the triads in all 12 keys. As we've seen already, some of these keys are not that common on the ukulele, but having this table here as a reference could be useful from time to time.

KEY	I	II	III	IV	V	VI	VII
C	C	Dm	Em	F	G	Am	Bdim
F	F	Gm	Am	Bb	C	Dm	Edim
Bb	Bb	Cm	Dm	Eb	F	Gm	Adim
Eb	Eb	Fm	Gm	Ab	Bb	Cm	Ddim
Ab	Ab	Bbm	Cm	Db	Eb	Fm	Gdim
Db	Db	Ebm	Fm	Gb	Ab	Bbm	Cdim
Gb	Gb	Abm	Bbm	Cb	Db	Ebm	Fdim
B	B	C#m	D#m	E	F#	G#m	A#dim
E	E	F#m	G#m	A	B	C#m	D#dim
A	A	Bm	C#m	D	E	F#m	G#dim
D	D	Em	F#m	G	A	Bm	C#dim
G	G	Am	Bm	C	D	Em	F#dim

Don't forget that if you take the roots of all the chords in any key you get the notes in the 'parent' major scale!

Appendix 2:
Notes on the Ukulele

This diagram shows you all the notes on the ukulele fretboard. Notice how the 'musical alphabet' is laid out on each string, just starting from a different note on each.

I've only shown one of the possible names for each flat/sharp note here, but remember, each flat/sharp note has two names used to refer to it!

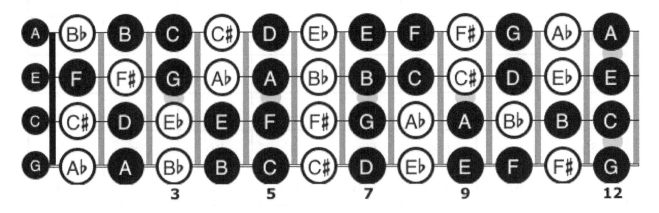

Appendix 3:
Complete Chord / Key Chart
for Minor Keys

This table shows you the chords in all the minor keys. Only the 'standard' chords from the natural minor scale are shown here. Don't forget, we often use 'stand-in chords' in minor keys so be aware of which chords will often change in these keys!

KEY	I	II	III	IV	V	VI	VII
A minor	Am	Bdim	C	Dm	Em	F	G
E minor	Em	F#dim	G	Am	Bm	C	D
D minor	Dm	Edim	F	Gm	Am	B*b*	C
G minor	Gm	Adim	B*b*	Cm	Dm	E*b*	F
B minor	Bm	C#dim	D	Em	F#m	G	A
C minor	Cm	Ddim	E*b*	Fm	Gm	A*b*	B*b*
F minor	Fm	Gdim	A*b*	B*b*m	Cm	Dd	E*b*
F# minor	F#m	G#dim	A	Bm	C#m	D	E
C# minor	C#m	D#dim	E	F#m	G#m	A	B
B*b* minor	B*b*m	Cdim	D*b*	E*b*m	Fm	G*b*	A*b*
E*b* minor	E*b*m	Fdim	G*b*	A*b*m	B*b*m	C*b*	D*b*
G# minor	G#m	A#dim	B	C#m	D#m	E	F#

Appendix 4:
Useful Chord Shapes

On the following pages are some of the most useful major, minor and dominant7 chord shapes found on the ukulele.

This is not supposed to be an exhaustive look at ukulele chord shapes!

There are hundreds of other chord shapes besides these, but this gives you a handy reference source for many of the most commonly used chords.

Major Chord Shapes

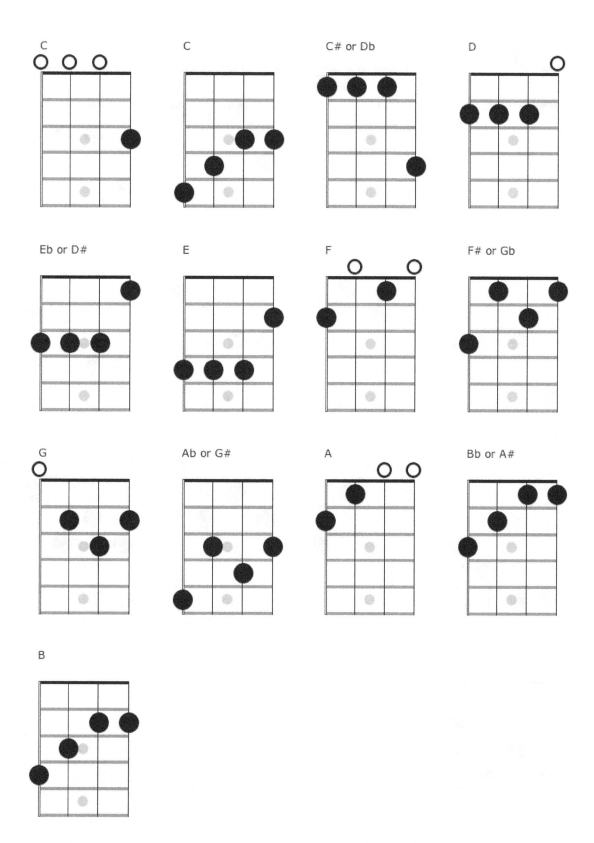

Minor Chord Shapes

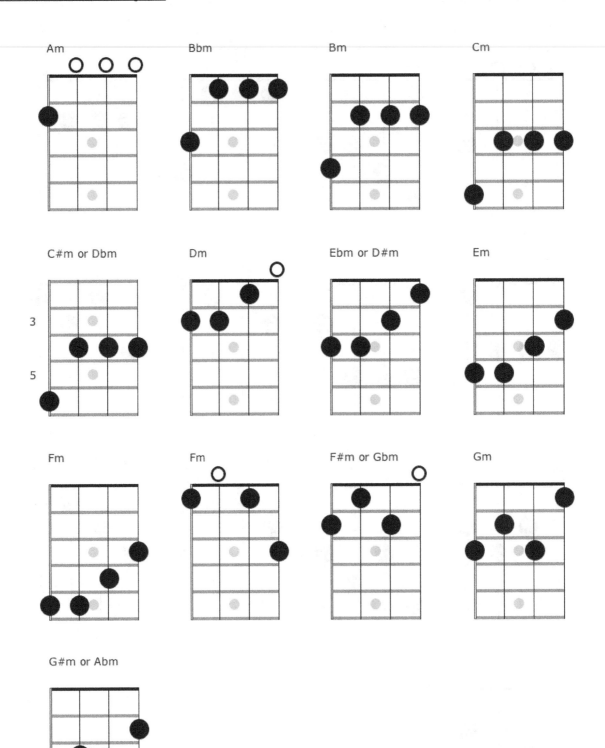

7 Chord Shapes ('Dominant7th' chords)

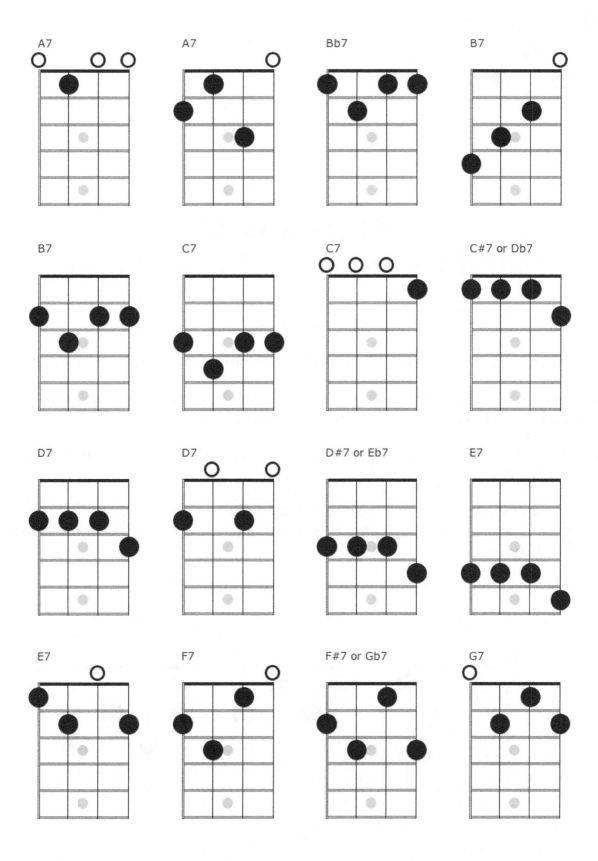

G#7 or Ab7

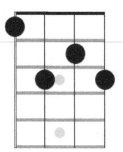

Appendix 5: 'Diminished 7th' Chord Shapes

These chords sometimes come in handy and sound great on the uke!

As the name suggests, they are related to the diminished triads we've seen in this book.

They are however slightly more complex, containing 4 notes instead of 3. Don't let this worry you, just learn the names and use them when necessary.

Normally when a chord symbol 'dim' is used ('C dim', 'G dim' etc), you'll need to use one of these chord shapes.

Notice how any *one* chord shape can be used to play **4** diminished chords. This makes diminished chords pretty easy; learn just 3 shapes and you can play any of the 12 possible diminished chords ...

Of course, make sure you know which shape to use for each one!

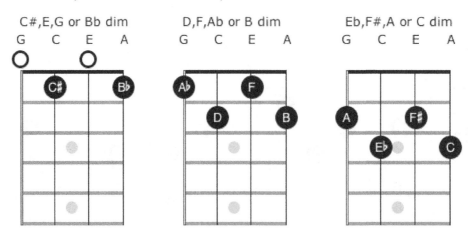

Music Theory for Ukulele
by David Shipway

Published by Headstock Books
headstockbooks.com

Cover images by Samuel Ramos and Jakob Owens.

Paperback ISBN: 978-1-914453-50-2
Hardcover ISBN: 978-1-914453-52-6 / 978-1-914453-53-3
Ebook ISBN: 978-1-914453-51-9

Made in the USA
Monee, IL
21 February 2024

53872665R00066